GENTLE TAI CHI FOR SENIORS

Simple Daily Routines to Improve Balance, Strength, and Flexibility—
Prevent Falls, Ease Joint Pain, and Boost Longevity

HANNAH HARMONY

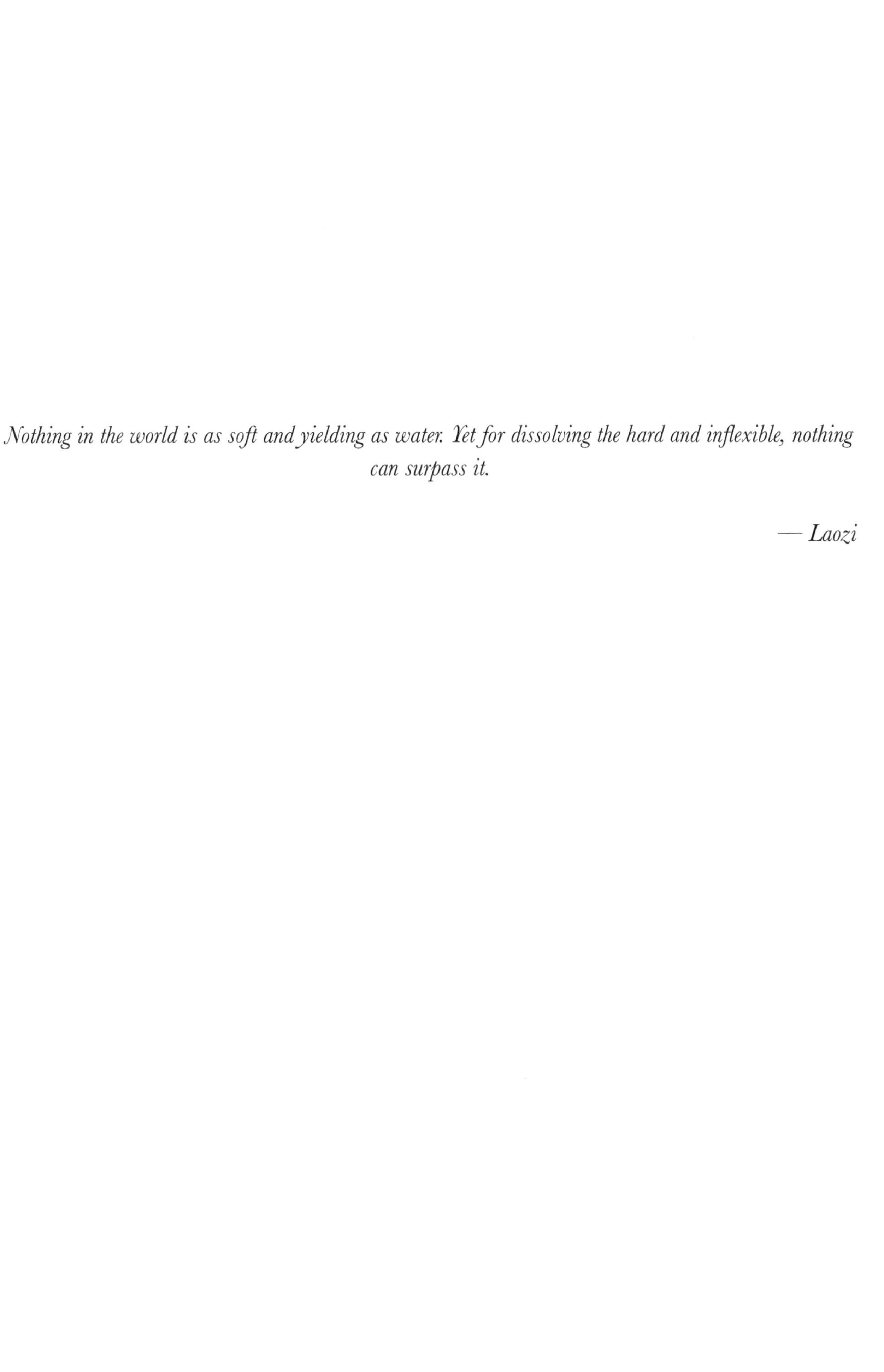

Nothing in the world is as soft and yielding as water. Yet for dissolving the hard and inflexible, nothing can surpass it.

— Laozi

Contents

Introduction   vii

Part 1: Getting Started with Gentle Tai Chi

1. The Story of Tai Chi, A Gift from Ancient Times   3
2. What Is Tai Chi?   5
3. Why Tai Chi Is Perfect for Seniors   8
4. Before You Begin   10

Part 2: The Gentle Tai Chi Exercise Library

5. Foundation and Posture   15
6. Balance and Coordination   30
7. Strength and Flexibility   45
8. Calm and Breathing   60
9. Joint Relief and Accessibility   75

Part 3: The 28-Day Gentle Tai Chi Challenge

10. How to Follow the Challenge   93
11. Your 28-Day Plan Overview   95
12. Week 1 – Gentle Awareness (Days 1–7)   97
13. Week 2 – Building Strength and Stability (Days 8–14)   99
14. Week 3 – Flow and Coordination (Days 15–21)   101
15. Week 4 – Calm and Renewal (Days 22–28)   103
16. After the 28 Days   104

Part 4: Continuing the Journey

17. Keep Moving Forward   107
18. Living the Tai Chi Way   108

Part 5: Resources and Support

Appendix A: Quick Reference Exercise Index   111
Appendix B: Seated 10-Minute Routine (For Rest or Recovery Days)   114
Appendix C: Frequently Asked Questions   116

Conclusion: A Note from the Author   119
References   121

Introduction

A Gentle Path to Strength and Balance

If you are reading this, it's likely because you want to move more freely, feel steadier on your feet, and stay active without pushing your body too hard. You may be searching for something that helps you stay healthy without pain, exhaustion, or strain. You might even miss the days when getting up from a chair or climbing a few steps didn't take so much effort. The good news is that you can still move with strength, balance, and grace, no matter your age. This book is here to help you do exactly that.

Tai Chi is not about being fast, flexible, or athletic. It's about being *present*; feeling your body, calming your mind, and allowing gentle movement to bring you energy and peace. This practice has been passed down for hundreds of years, originally developed as a martial art but later refined into a slow, flowing form of exercise that anyone can do.

For older adults, Tai Chi is especially powerful. Research shows that it improves balance, strengthens the legs, supports joint health, and reduces the risk of falls. But beyond the science, what makes Tai Chi truly special is how it makes you *feel*. It slows the rush of the day, eases the tension in your shoulders, and gives you back a sense of control over your body.

This book was created with you in mind. You don't need to have any experience, and you don't need to be flexible or strong to start. You only need curiosity, a bit of patience, and ten minutes a day.

Many people begin Tai Chi thinking they will only improve their balance but end up uncovering so much more. They find peace of mind, deeper breathing, and a renewed sense of confidence in everyday movement. That is the beauty of this practice; it works gently, from the inside out.

As you begin your journey, remember: Tai Chi is not about perfection; it's about progress, comfort, and calm. Whether you are standing tall or sitting in a chair, every movement you make counts.

How to Use This Book (Skip, Scan, or Follow Along)

You can use this book however you like. It was designed to be flexible and easy to follow, so you can go at your own pace.

If you enjoy structure, you can follow the **Twenty-Eight-Day Gentle Tai Chi Challenge** in Part Three, where each day has a short routine that builds your balance and confidence over time. If you prefer to explore, you can skip ahead to the **Exercise Library** in Part Two, which contains thirty-five different exercises you can pick and choose from.

Each exercise includes:

- **Step-by-step instructions** written in simple, clear language.
- **Reference images** so you can see exactly how to move.
- **Accessible versions** for seated or standing positions.
- **Duration and repetitions** so you know how long to practice.
- **Benefits** to help you understand what each exercise supports.

If you ever feel tired or need to rest, that is completely fine. Tai Chi isn't about doing it all; it's about *doing what feels right for you*. Some days you might feel full of energy and ready to complete the full routine, while other days you might only do one or two movements. Both are perfectly okay.

You can also simply flip through the book and try whatever catches your eye. Some people like to read the explanations first; others jump right into the exercises.

This is *your* Tai Chi journey. Whether you choose to follow it page by page or skip around, you will still gain strength, calm, and confidence as you move.

As we grow older, our bodies change. Our joints may ache, our steps may become smaller, and our balance may feel less certain. But aging does not mean stopping; it means moving in a way that *supports* the body we have now.

Tai Chi meets you where you are. You don't need to keep up with anyone else, and you won't find complicated routines here. The exercises are slow, smooth, and mindful. They are designed to strengthen your body safely while keeping your joints happy.

Think of Tai Chi as "moving meditation." Each motion flows into the next, teaching you to breathe and move at the same time. As you move, your muscles and joints loosen, your breathing deepens, and your mind relaxes.

Here are just a few ways Tai Chi can support you:

- **Better balance and fewer falls:** Tai Chi strengthens the muscles around your ankles, knees, and hips, which are key for stability. You'll feel more confident walking, turning, and reaching.
- **Improved flexibility:** Gentle stretching and circular movements help release stiffness in the neck, shoulders, and back.
- **Pain relief:** Regular movement keeps your joints lubricated and your muscles relaxed, which may ease arthritis and back pain.
- **Calmer mind and better mood:** The breathing and rhythm of Tai Chi help lower stress and improve sleep. Many people say they feel lighter and more at peace after practicing.
- **Increased energy:** Even though it is gentle, Tai Chi gets your blood flowing and helps you feel more awake and alive.

It's also an exercise you can do anywhere: in your living room, your backyard, or even while sitting in a chair. You don't need fancy equipment, gym clothes, or a big space. You just need a few minutes each day to reconnect with your body.

This book will guide you through simple steps that build over time. You will start small, with easy movements, and slowly grow stronger and more balanced with each day of practice.

Remember, this is not a race. It's a gentle path, one that respects where you are today and helps you move toward where you want to be tomorrow.

One of the best things about Tai Chi is that you don't need much to get started.

Here is all you need:

- **A safe, open space:** Find an area where you can move your arms and legs freely. A clear space in your living room, patio, or bedroom works perfectly.
- **A sturdy chair:** This can be used for support or to sit on during seated exercises. Make sure it does not roll or swivel.
- **Comfortable clothing:** Wear something loose and soft that allows for easy movement.
- **Flat, supportive shoes or bare feet:** Many people prefer soft-soled shoes, but barefoot practice is also fine if the surface is safe and stable.
- **Good lighting:** Make sure you can see clearly, especially if you are following the illustrations.
- **Optional:** A water bottle and a small towel, in case you warm up.

That's it. No weights, no mats, no gym. Just you, your breath, and a few quiet minutes to move gently.

You can practice at any time of day. Some people like to begin their morning with Tai Chi to feel more awake, while others prefer it in the evening to relax before bed. Try both and see which feels better for you.

If you live with someone, you might even enjoy doing the exercises together. Moving side by side can make it more fun and motivating.

A NOTE ON SAFETY AND COMFORT

Before starting any exercise routine, it's always a good idea to check with your doctor, especially if you have joint pain, high blood pressure, heart issues, or balance problems. Tai Chi is gentle, but safety always comes first.

During practice, remember these simple rules:

- **Move slowly:** There is no rush. Tai Chi isn't about speed.
- **Listen to your body:** If something feels painful, stop and rest. Gentle stretching should feel good, not sharp or uncomfortable.

- **Keep your posture soft:** Avoid locking your knees or tensing your shoulders.
- **Breathe naturally:** Never hold your breath; let your breath guide your pace.
- **Use support when needed:** It's perfectly okay to hold the back of a chair or rest between exercises.

If you ever feel dizzy, short of breath, or off balance, pause and sit down. You can resume when you feel ready.

You may notice that your body feels different on different days. Some days you might move easily, while other days your joints may feel tight. This is completely normal; what matters is consistency. The more regularly you practice, the more comfortable and capable you will feel.

Think of Tai Chi as something you can grow with. Over time, you will move more smoothly, breathe more deeply, and trust your balance more. You will also feel more confident doing daily activities like climbing stairs, carrying groceries, or simply walking outdoors.

A FINAL WORD BEFORE YOU BEGIN

This book is not about doing things perfectly; it's about taking gentle, meaningful steps toward better health. It's about feeling proud of yourself for showing up, even for ten minutes a day.

You won't just be exercising; you will be reconnecting with your body, breath, and balance. Every small movement is a step toward strength and confidence.

So take a deep breath. Roll your shoulders. Smile. You are about to begin something wonderful, something that will help you move with more ease, stand a little taller, and feel more alive. Welcome to your gentle Tai Chi journey.

Part 1: Getting Started with Gentle Tai Chi

A Clear and Supportive Beginning for Seniors

This part of the book is designed to help you begin gently and with confidence. If you are new to Tai Chi, or if movement feels uncertain right now, you are in the right place. You don't need any experience, special equipment, or a high fitness level to get started.

Part One explains what Tai Chi is in simple, easy-to-understand language and shows you how to prepare for safe, comfortable practice. You will learn why slow, mindful movement is especially helpful as we age, and how Tai Chi can support balance, posture, breathing, and calm without strain.

You will also find guidance on how to use this book in a way that feels right for you. There is no need to read everything in order or remember every detail. You can move at your own pace, return to sections when needed, and choose what feels helpful.

This section also covers simple breathing tips, how to set up a safe practice space, and how to choose between seated and standing options. Most importantly, it reminds you that Tai Chi is meant to feel kind and supportive.

Take your time with this part. When you feel ready, you can move forward knowing you have a gentle and solid foundation to build upon.

CHAPTER 1: THE STORY OF TAI CHI, A GIFT FROM ANCIENT TIMES

Long ago, nestled among the misty Wudang Mountains of China, lived a wise monk named Zhang Sanfeng. Legend says that one afternoon, while looking out from his quiet retreat, he witnessed a most unusual sight: a fight between a graceful crane and a clever snake.

The crane attacked with its sharp beak and powerful wings, but the snake did not try to match the bird's strength with its own. Instead, the snake moved in smooth, circular patterns, simply flowing out of the way of every strike. No matter how hard the crane lunged, it couldn't land a blow because the snake was too supple and relaxed.

Watching this, Zhang Sanfeng had a "lightbulb moment." He realized that softness can overcome hardness and that moving with nature, rather than against it, is where true strength lies. He began to develop a series of movements that mimicked that same flowing, balanced energy.

What's in a Name?

You might wonder what the words "Tai Chi" actually mean. In the original Chinese, the full name is *Tai Chi Chuan*:

- **Tai (太):** Means "Supreme" or "Grand."
- **Chi (极):** Means "Ultimate" or the "Highest Point."
- **Chuan (拳):** Means "Fist" or "Movement."

Together, it is often translated as "Supreme Ultimate Movement." It represents the vastness of the universe and the perfect balance between two opposite forces: Yin and Yang (like rest and action, or soft and firm).

While Tai Chi began as a specialized martial art in the seventeenth century within the Chen Village, it eventually evolved into the gentle health practice we love today. Masters like Yang Luchan recognized that these slow, mindful movements weren't just for self-defense; they were a powerful way to keep the body strong, the joints flexible, and the mind calm at any age.

Today, millions of people around the world practice Tai Chi to improve their balance and vitality. As you begin the exercises in this book, remember the crane and the snake: you don't need to use brute force to be strong. By moving gently and breathing deeply, you are tapping into a centuries-old tradition of wellness.

CHAPTER 2: WHAT IS TAI CHI?

A Simple Introduction to an Ancient Practice

Tai Chi is an ancient form of exercise that began in China hundreds of years ago. Even if it is old, it's still one of the safest and most effective ways for older adults to stay active. You may have seen people in parks moving slowly, almost like they are flowing through water. That gentle, steady movement is Tai Chi.

Think of Tai Chi as a moving meditation. You are not rushing. You are not pushing yourself or forcing anything. Instead, you are allowing your body to glide from one soft movement to another while breathing calmly and staying aware of your balance. Many seniors love Tai Chi because it doesn't feel harsh or painful. It doesn't require you to get on the floor, lift heavy weights, or move fast. You don't need special equipment. You only need a little space, a comfortable chair, and a willingness to move slowly.

The reason Tai Chi has been practiced for so long is that it works. It supports the body, calms the mind, and gives people of all ages a way to feel strong and centered again. Even if you haven't exercised in years, Tai Chi welcomes you exactly where you are.

Tai Chi and Qigong: What Is the Difference?

You may hear the words Tai Chi and Qigong mentioned together. They look similar and feel similar, so it's natural to wonder what the difference is.

You can think of Tai Chi and Qigong as close relatives. Both involve slow movements, calm breathing, and gentle focus. Both improve balance and reduce stress. Both are safe for seniors and absolute beginners.

The difference is simple. Qigong movements are usually shorter, easier, and more repetitive. Tai Chi routines can sometimes be longer or have more flowing sequences.

In this book, you will learn gentle Tai Chi movements that are simple enough to feel like Qigong, but still give you the full benefit of Tai Chi. Whether you call it Tai Chi or Qigong, the goal is the same: you will strengthen your body, calm your mind, and feel steadier on your feet.

The Gentle Power of Slow Movement

Many people think exercise must be fast or sweaty to be effective. Tai Chi proves the opposite. Slow movement can be powerful. When you move slowly, your muscles must support you in a steady and controlled way. This builds strength without strain. Your mind also stays more aware of your posture, your balance, and your breathing.

Here is a simple example. If you lift your foot quickly, you barely feel anything. But if you raise your foot slowly, your leg muscles begin to work. You feel your weight shift, you stay aware of your balance. That is the gentle strength of Tai Chi. Every movement quietly trains the body to stay stable and calm.

This is one reason Tai Chi is so helpful for seniors. It strengthens without hurting. It calms without making you feel tired. It teaches your body to stay balanced even during everyday activities like stepping up a curb, walking up stairs, or reaching for something on a shelf.

What to Expect as a Beginner

Starting Tai Chi doesn't require any special background. You don't need to be flexible or athletic, and you don't need to memorize long routines. All you need is a desire to move gently each day.

As a beginner, you can expect:

- Movements that are slow and comfortable.
- Exercises that can be done seated or standing.
- Time to learn at your own pace.
- No pressure to be perfect.
- More confidence with each session.

Many seniors start Tai Chi after an injury, after a fall, or simply because they want to feel steadier. Others start because they want to ease stiffness in their back, hips, or shoulders, or even because they want to feel more peaceful inside. Whatever your reason, Tai Chi meets you exactly where you are.

You will begin with small steps. With each day, the movements will feel more natural. You may notice that simple actions like turning your head, stepping sideways, or bending to pick up an object feel easier. You may breathe more fully and sleep more deeply. You may feel calmer during the day.

This book will guide you gently through everything. You will never be rushed. You will never be asked to do anything that feels unsafe. Every movement has an accessible version, so you can always choose what feels right for your body.

CHAPTER 3: WHY TAI CHI IS PERFECT FOR SENIORS

The Physical Benefits: Strength, Flexibility, and Balance

Tai Chi is especially helpful for seniors because it improves the parts of the body that often weaken with age. You will strengthen your legs, core, and back. You will loosen your joints. You will improve your balance and coordination. These are exactly the areas that support independence as you get older.

Here are a few simple examples:

- When you shift your weight slowly from one leg to the other, your legs and core become stronger.
- When you turn your torso gently, your spine becomes more flexible.
- When you move your arms in slow circles, your shoulders become looser and more relaxed.
- When you breathe with awareness, your body receives more oxygen, and your energy increases.

Many seniors fear falling as they age. Tai Chi directly supports balance. The slow shifting of weight teaches your body how to stay centered. This helps you feel more stable as you walk, stand up, or step sideways. Studies show that Tai Chi reduces the risk of falls in older adults, even for those with previous injuries.

Another important benefit is improved posture. Many seniors slowly begin to hunch forward without noticing it. Tai Chi encourages an upright and relaxed posture. Standing tall helps your breathing, digestion, and circulation.

The Emotional Benefits: Calm, Focus, and Confidence

Tai Chi benefits the mind just as much as the body. The slow, rhythmic movements are soothing. They quiet the mind and help release tension. Many people find that their worries feel lighter after a session.

Tai Chi can help with:

- Stress and anxiety.
- Mental fog.
- Emotional tension.
- Difficulty sleeping.
- Feeling overwhelmed.

Because the movements are gentle and enjoyable, the practice becomes something to look forward to rather than something that feels like work. Seniors often say that Tai Chi gives them a peaceful moment during the day; it becomes a time to breathe, move, and reconnect with their body in a kind and patient way.

Confidence is another important benefit. When you notice yourself moving more easily, standing more steadily, or feeling more comfortable reaching or bending, your confidence grows. You begin to trust your body again, even if years of stiffness or fear of falling have held you back.

The Mind-Body Connection

Tai Chi teaches you to move with awareness. Your mind pays attention to each shift, each breath, and each soft turn of the body. This connection between your mind and your body improves coordination, reaction time, and overall awareness.

Think of it as learning to listen to your body again. You notice when your weight shifts. You feel when a muscle is tight or when your breath becomes slow. This makes everyday movements safer because you are more aware of how your body responds.

Real Results in Just Ten Minutes a Day

You don't need long workouts to benefit from Tai Chi; ten minutes a day is enough. In that short time, you can gently improve strength, balance, and flexibility while giving your joints a chance to move without strain. You help your muscles stay active and calm your mind for the rest of the day.

Small steps make a big difference when done consistently. Many seniors are surprised by how much better they feel after just two or three weeks of regular practice. Movement becomes easier, stiffness lighter, and balance steadier. A simple daily ten-minute commitment can bring real change.

CHAPTER 4: BEFORE YOU BEGIN

How to Prepare Your Practice Space

You don't need a large space to do Tai Chi. A small, safe, and quiet corner is enough. Here is how to prepare:

- Choose a flat, clear area with enough space to move your arms gently.
- Make sure the floor is not slippery.
- Remove small rugs that might slide.
- Have a sturdy chair nearby if you want to use it for support or seated exercises.
- If possible, choose a spot with good lighting.
- Wear comfortable clothes that allow for easy movement.

Some seniors enjoy practicing near a window so they can look outside, while others prefer quiet music or even practicing in silence. Choose what feels peaceful to you.

What to Wear and What to Avoid

You don't need athletic clothing. You simply need clothes that feel comfortable and loose enough for movement. Soft pants, a simple shirt, or anything you wear around the house is fine. Shoes should be supportive but flexible. Some seniors practice in socks if the floor is not slippery, but most prefer soft-soled shoes for stability.

Avoid clothing that is too tight, shoes with thick, heavy soles, or anything that restricts your movements.

Breathing Basics for Relaxation

Breathing is an important part of Tai Chi. You don't need to breathe in any special or complicated way. Simply breathe slowly and naturally. Here is a calm way to begin:

- Inhale gently through your nose.

- Allow your belly to soften.
- Exhale slowly through your mouth.
- Let your shoulders relax.

Breathing like this helps your body release tension. It signals your mind that you are safe and calm. It also brings more oxygen to your muscles, which helps them move more easily.

WARM-UP AND COOL-DOWN MINI ROUTINES (THREE TO FIVE MINUTES EACH)

Before beginning your exercises, it is helpful to gently warm up your body. After your session, you can cool down with a few calming movements.

Warm Up (3 minutes)

- Roll your shoulders slowly forward and back.
- Gently turn your head side to side.
- Lift your arms slowly to shoulder height and lower them.
- Shift your weight lightly from one foot to the other.

Cool Down (3 minutes)

- Place your hands on your belly and breathe slowly.
- Let your arms float up and then down gently.
- Relax your shoulders and soften your posture.
- Sit down if needed and breathe until you feel calm and steady.

These mini routines prepare your body for movement and help prevent stiffness afterward.

SEATED OR STANDING? CHOOSE WHAT WORKS FOR YOU

All movements in this book can be done either seated or standing. Both options are equally valuable. Standing helps build balance and leg strength, while seated movements help you stay safe and steady if standing feels difficult.

Here are a few simple guidelines:

- If you feel unsteady, begin seated.
- If your knees or hips hurt, start seated and gradually build up to standing.
- If you are comfortable standing but feel tired halfway through, switch to seated movements.
- If you have a walker or cane, keep it nearby.

There is no right or wrong choice; the goal is to move your body safely and gently. You may even switch between seated and standing versions as your confidence grows. Listening to your body is the most important part of Tai Chi.

Part 2: The Gentle Tai Chi Exercise Library

A SIMPLE GUIDE TO MOVING SAFELY AND CONFIDENTLY

This part of the book is your personal Tai Chi exercise library. You can think of it as a collection of gentle movements that help your body feel stronger, looser, and more balanced. You don't need to memorize anything. You can flip through the pages, try one exercise at a time, or repeat the ones you enjoy most. There is no wrong way to use this section.

Every exercise in this library includes clear step-by-step instructions, simple images you can follow, and an accessible seated version for days when standing feels difficult. You will also see the benefits listed so you can choose exercises that match how you feel each day. For example, you might pick movements that help with joint stiffness in the morning or choose calming exercises before bedtime.

Move slowly, breathe gently, and listen to your body. Even small movements can improve how you feel.

CHAPTER 5: FOUNDATION AND POSTURE

Building Strength From the Ground Up

Chapter Five focuses on the most important part of your Tai Chi practice: your foundation. These exercises teach you how to stand, sit, and move in a way that feels steady and effortless. You will learn how to align your posture, relax your shoulders, shift your weight safely, and feel grounded in your body.

These gentle movements are perfect for beginners, seniors with limited mobility, or anyone who wants to build confidence before trying more flowing Tai Chi sequences. You can practice all of them standing or seated. The goal is not perfection; it's to help your body feel supported, upright, and calm.

Start with the exercises that feel most comfortable and take your time. With each breath and each gentle movement, your strength and balance will grow.

Focus: Calm, grounding, and gentle warm-up.

Benefits:
This movement helps relax your nervous system, lower tension, and prepare your body for Tai Chi. It improves breathing capacity, reduces stress, and helps you feel more balanced and aware of your posture.

Duration: 1 to 2 minutes.
Repetitions: 6 to 10 slow breaths.

Steps:

1. Stand or sit upright with your feet flat and relaxed.
2. Place one hand on your belly and the other on your chest.
3. Close your eyes and gently inhale through your nose. Feel your belly rise under your hand.
4. Exhale slowly through your mouth. Let your shoulders soften.
5. Keep your eyes closed or softly lowered.
6. Continue breathing slowly, feeling your body become still and centered.

Accessible Version (Seated):

Sit in a sturdy chair with your feet flat on the ground. Keep your back supported or unsupported, depending on your comfort level, and follow the steps above.

Before/After Notes:

Do this before any exercise to calm your body. After movement sessions, use this breath to cool down and release tension.

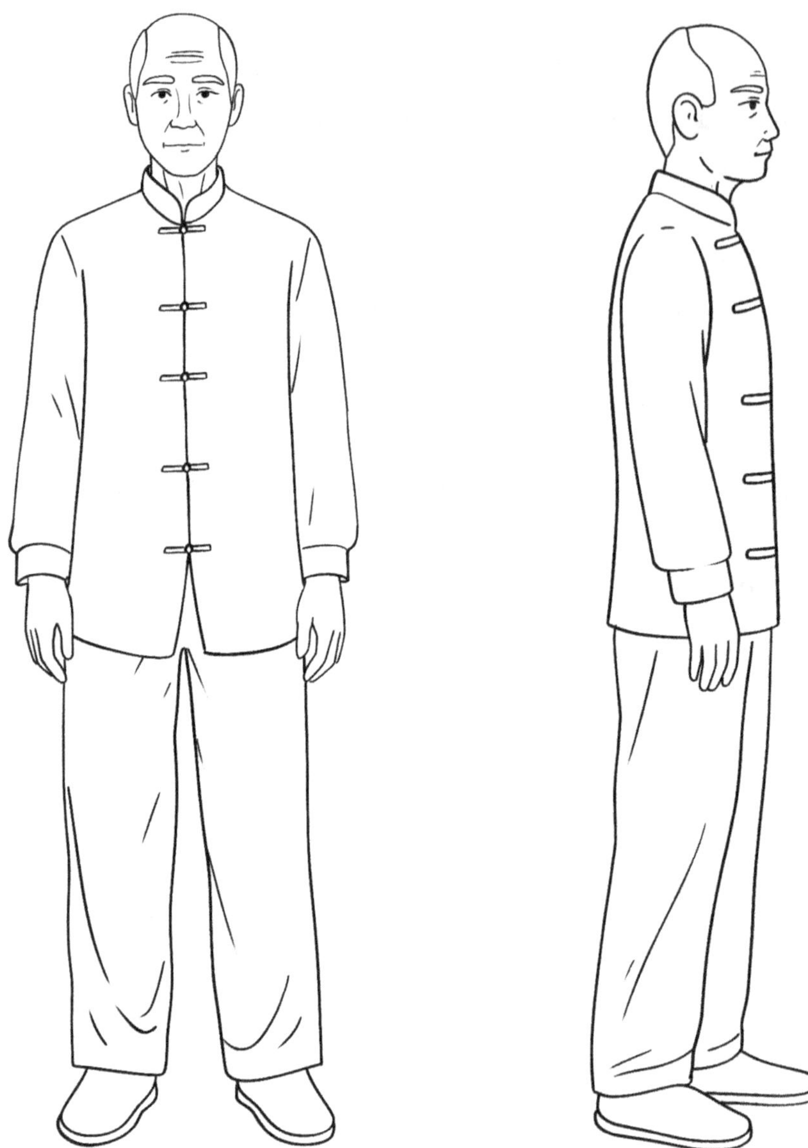

Focus: Posture, grounding, and stability.

Benefits:
Mountain Stance improves posture, strengthens the legs gently, and teaches your body how to stand tall without tension. It also increases body awareness and reduces slouching.

Duration: 1 minute.

Repetitions: Hold for 20 to 30 seconds, repeat twice.

Steps:

1. Stand with your feet hip-width apart.
2. Keep your knees slightly bent but not locked.
3. Let your arms hang loosely by your sides.
4. Lift the top of your head gently upward, lengthening your spine.
5. Relax your shoulders and soften your jaw.
6. Breathe slowly as you hold this calm, tall posture.

Accessible Version (Seated):
Sit at the front of your chair with your feet flat on the ground. Lengthen your spine and relax your arms at your sides.

Before/After Notes:
Use this movement before exercises that require balance to help establish a steady, grounded base. Afterward, take a moment to notice your posture and breathing before transitioning into the next movement.

3. Seated Posture Alignment

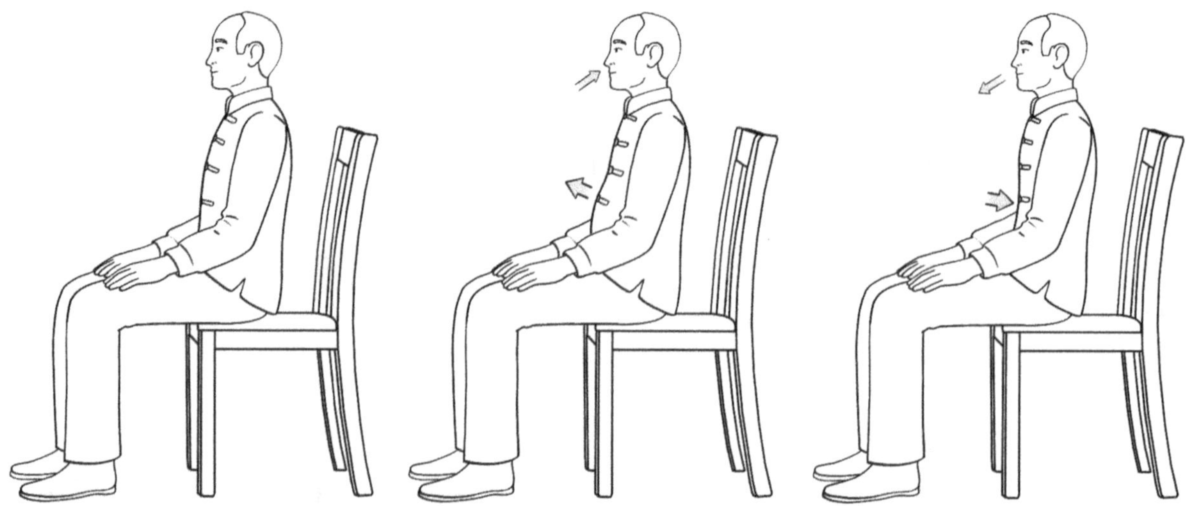

Focus: Safe seated practice and posture control.

Benefits:

This movement helps reduce back discomfort, support easier breathing, and create a comfortable seated foundation for Tai Chi practice. It encourages an upright posture, improves body awareness, and helps seniors feel more stable and at ease while seated.

Duration: 1 minute.
Repetitions: Hold for 20 seconds, reset, and repeat twice.

Steps:

1. Sit toward the front of a sturdy chair.
2. Place your feet flat on the ground and hip-width apart.
3. Lengthen your spine upward as if a string is lifting your head.
4. Relax your shoulders and keep your hands resting on your thighs.
5. Keep your chin level.
6. Breathe slowly to settle into your alignment.

Accessible Version:

All versions are accessible; you may place a cushion behind your back for support.

Before/After Notes:
Use this alignment before any seated exercise to create a comfortable, upright foundation for movement. Afterward, allow your shoulders to soften and notice how steady and supported your posture feels.

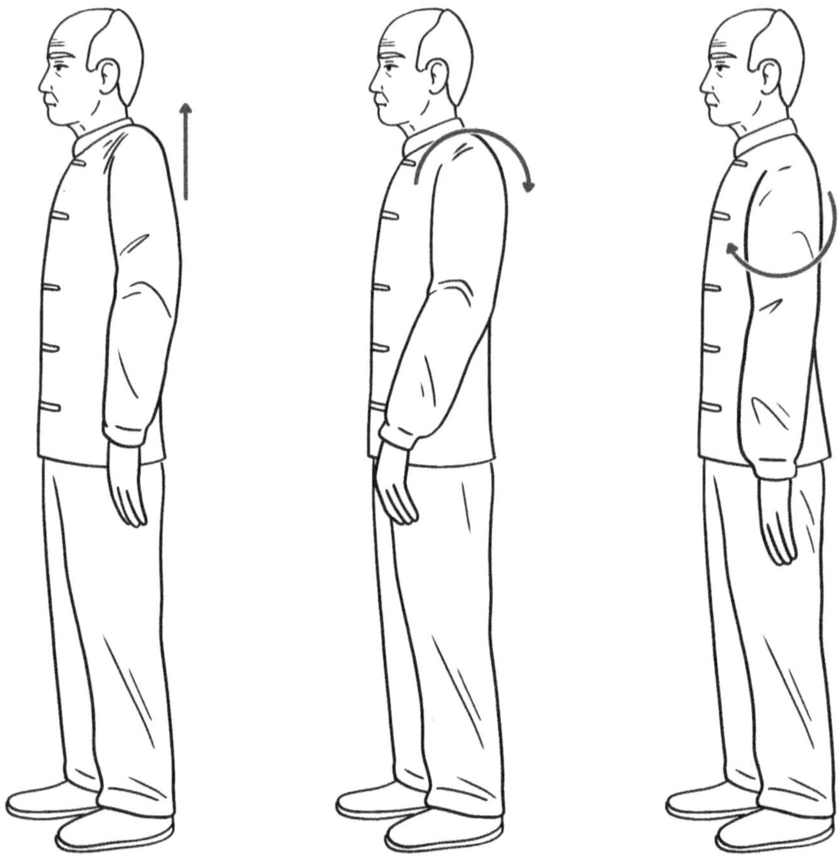

Focus: Loosening tension in the shoulders and upper back.

Benefits:
This movement helps release shoulder stiffness, reduce neck tension, and gently prepare the upper body for movement. It improves shoulder mobility, supports relaxed posture, and encourages smoother, more comfortable motion.

Duration: 1 to 2 minutes.
Repetitions: 10 rolls forward, 10 rolls backward.

Steps:

1. Stand or sit tall.
2. Slowly lift both shoulders upward.

3. Roll them gently back and downward.
4. Repeat in a smooth circular motion.
5. After 10 backward circles, roll your shoulders forward for 10 circles.
6. Keep breathing softly throughout.

Accessible Version (Seated):

Sit comfortably with your feet flat on the ground. Perform the same shoulder circles.

Before/After Notes:

Use this movement as a gentle warm-up at the start of a Tai Chi session to loosen your shoulders and upper body. Afterward, allow your shoulders to settle and notice any release of tension before continuing.

5. Open the Chest and Breathe

Focus: Chest mobility and ease of breathing.

Benefits:
This movement helps open the chest, reduce tightness in the upper torso, and encourage deeper, more comfortable breathing. It improves breathing capacity, supports better posture, and promotes a calm, relaxed feeling in the upper body.

Duration: 1 minute.
Repetitions: 8 to 12 repetitions.

Steps:

1. Stand or sit tall with your arms at your sides.
2. Inhale as you slowly open your arms wide, palms facing forward.
3. Gently lift your chest without arching your back.
4. Exhale as you bring your hands back down to your sides.
5. Move slowly and comfortably.

Accessible Version:

Seated movement is identical; keep the motions small if your shoulder mobility is limited.

Before/After Notes:

Use this movement as an energizing warm-up or a gentle cool-down to support open posture and easy breathing. Afterward, allow your arms to relax and notice a calm, refreshed feeling in your upper body before continuing.

Focus: Early balance training.

Benefits:
This movement helps gently strengthen the legs, improve balance, and increase awareness of weight transfer. It builds confidence in standing, supports steady movement, and helps reduce the fear of falling.

Duration: 1 minute.
Repetitions: 8 to 12 shifts per side.

Steps:

1. Stand with your feet hip-width apart.
2. Lower your hips and keep your knees soft, as if sitting on a high stool.
3. Slowly shift your weight to your left foot while fully extending your right leg to the side.
4. Keep your body upright without leaning.
5. Slowly shift your weight to your right foot as you extend your left leg.
6. Continue side to side with calm breathing.

Accessible Version:
Sit tall and shift your weight from your left hip to your right hip by gently pressing into each foot.

Before/After Notes:
Use this movement as a warm-up before standing sequences to gently prepare your body for shifting weight. Afterward, pause briefly to notice improved balance and a greater sense of ease when standing.

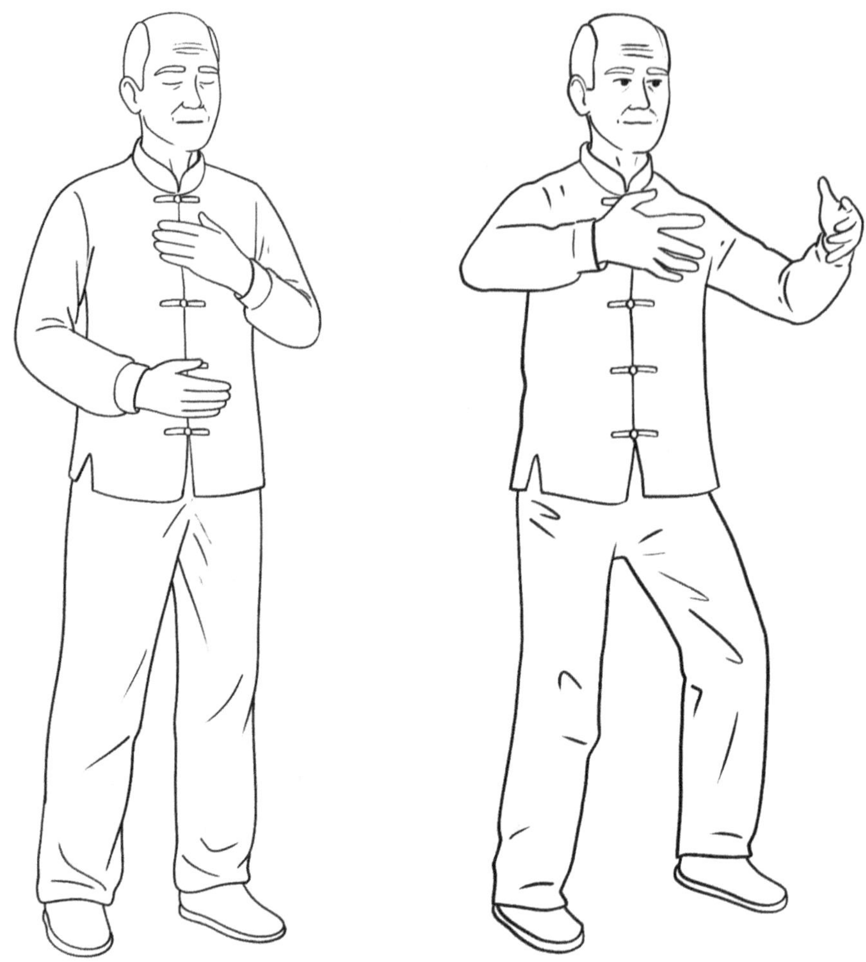

Focus: Grounding, leg strength, and calm focus.

Benefits:
This movement helps build stability through the legs, improve posture, and encourage a grounded, steady feeling. It gently increases leg endurance, supports balance, and helps seniors feel more secure and confident while standing.

Duration: 30 to 45 seconds.
Repetitions: Repeat 2 or 3 times.

Steps:

1. Stand tall with your feet shoulder-width apart.

2. Soften your knees so they are not locked.
3. Imagine your feet growing strong roots into the ground.
4. Keep your spine long, as if gently lifted from the top of your head.
5. Lift your arms in front of your chest, forming a soft circle as if you are holding a big ball.
6. Relax your shoulders and keep your hands loose.
7. Breathe in slowly through your nose and out gently through your mouth.
8. Hold the position for 30 to 45 seconds, staying calm and steady.

Accessible Version (Seated):
Sit tall with your feet wide and grounded. Keep your spine long and imagine your weight settling downward.

Before/After Notes:
Use this movement before balance exercises to help build confidence and a sense of stability. Afterward, take a moment to notice a grounded feeling through your feet and legs before moving on.

CHAPTER 6: BALANCE AND COORDINATION

This chapter focuses on movements that support steadier walking, smoother transitions, and better overall balance. Many seniors worry about losing stability or falling, and it's completely natural to feel cautious. Tai Chi offers a safe and gentle way to build confidence again without pushing your body too far. The exercises in this chapter use slow shifting of weight, soft arm motions, and coordinated steps that help your body learn how to stay steady during everyday activities.

You will notice that nothing in this chapter is rushed. Each exercise allows you to feel how your body moves, how your feet connect to the ground, and how your arms guide your balance instead of straining it. All movements can be done standing or seated, depending on what feels right for you. Whether you want to strengthen your balance, improve your coordination, or simply move with more ease, these exercises will help you build those skills gradually.

Take your time, breathe naturally, and remember that you never need to force a movement. Each small shift and gentle motion contributes to better stability over time. Think of this chapter as your soft, steady foundation for moving safely and confidently through your day.

8. Cloud Hands

Focus: Coordination, balance, and gentle flow.

Benefits:
This movement helps improve shoulder mobility, supports balanced side stepping, and encourages relaxed, flowing movement. It promotes coordination, calms the mind through rhythm, and helps the body move with greater ease and confidence.

Duration: 1 to 2 minutes.
Repetitions: 8 to 10 passes each direction.

Steps:

1. Stand with your feet hip-width apart.
2. Lift your left hand in front of your chest, palm facing inward.
3. Lower your right hand near your hip, palm facing the floor.
4. Gently glide your hands in opposite circles as you shift your weight to the left.
5. Switch your hands positions as you shift your weight to the right.
6. Continue moving your hands like drifting clouds.

Accessible Version:
The seated version uses the same arm movements without shifting the feet.

Before/After Notes:
Use this movement after more effortful exercises to help calm your mind and soften your body. Allow the motion to slow naturally at the end and return to relaxed, steady breathing before continuing.

9. WAVE THE HANDS LIKE WATER

Focus: Coordination and upper-body relaxation.

Benefits:
This movement helps soothe tight shoulders, encourage relaxation, and promote smooth, flowing movement. It improves coordination, enhances body awareness, and supports a calm, focused state of mind.

Duration: 1 minute.
Repetitions: 10 to 12 waves.

Steps:

1. Stand or sit tall.
2. Lift both hands gently in front of you at shoulder height.
3. Move your hands up and down like rolling waves.
4. Keep your wrists relaxed and soft.
5. Synchronize your movements with slow breaths.

Accessible Version:
The seated version is identical, keeping movement soft and flowing.

Before/After Notes:
Use this movement when you are feeling tension in your upper back or shoulders to encourage gentle release. Afterward, allow your arms to relax and notice a softer, more fluid feeling through your upper body before moving on.

10. STEPPING FORWARD WITH FLOW

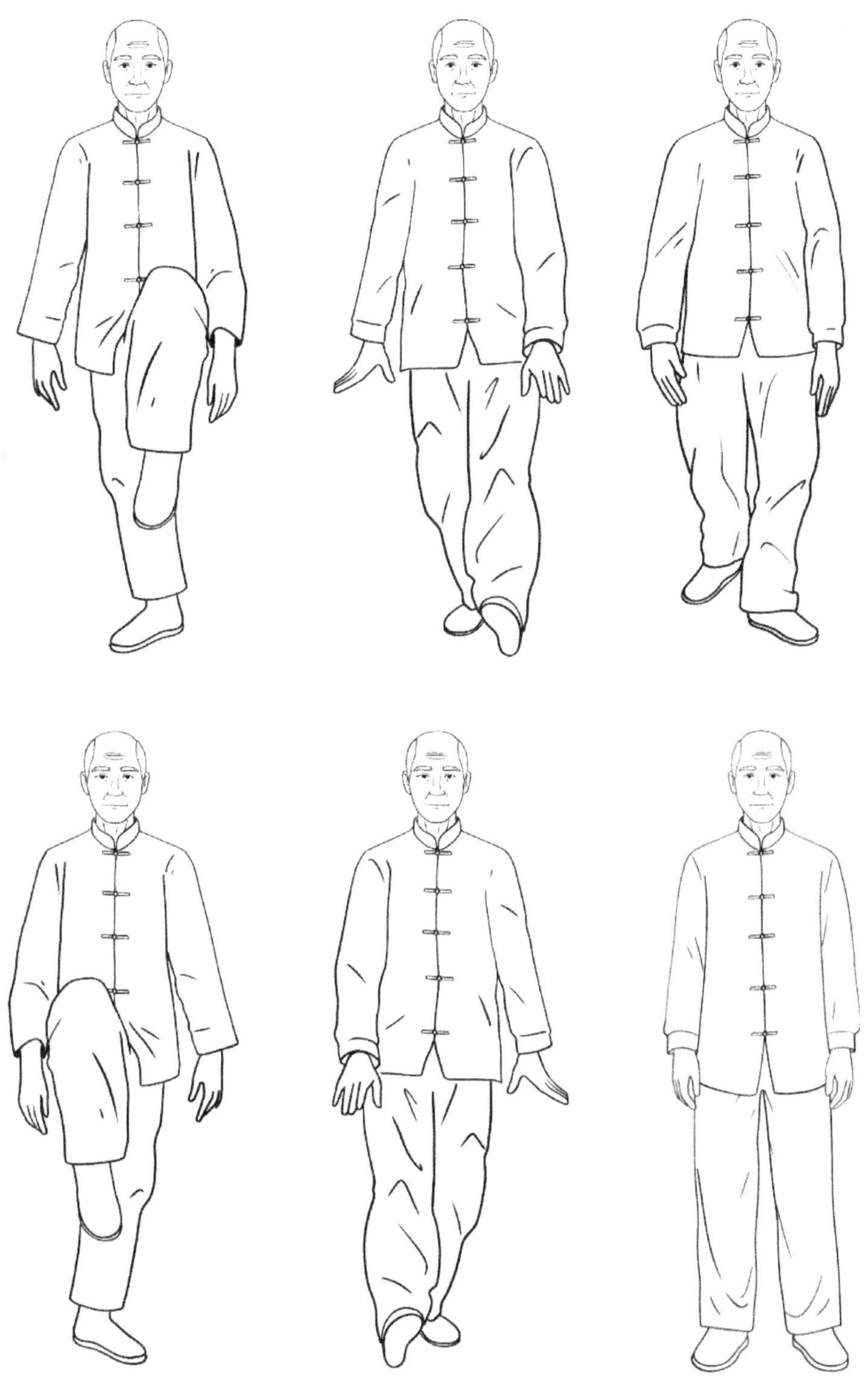

Focus: Safe forward stepping.

Benefits:
This movement helps improve walking confidence, gently strengthen the legs, and support smooth, coordinated stepping. It encourages ease when moving forward and helps reduce fear by promoting steady, controlled movement.

Duration: 1 minute.
Repetitions: 6 to 8 forward steps for each leg.

STEPS:

1. Stand with your feet hip-width apart.
2. Gently shift your weight to your right foot.
3. Softly step forward with your left foot.
4. Shift your weight onto the front foot.
5. Return slowly to your starting position.
6. Repeat on the other side.

Accessible Version:
The seated version mimics stepping motions by extending one foot forward and drawing it back.

Before/After Notes:
Use this movement before walking practice or balance training to prepare your legs and build confidence with forward stepping. Afterward, pause briefly to notice your steadiness and return to calm breathing before continuing.

Focus: Coordination of hands and legs.

Benefits:

This movement helps improve walking balance, gently strengthen the legs, and encourage calm, coordinated movement. It enhances focus, supports steady stepping, and promotes confidence during everyday walking.

Duration: 1 to 2 minutes.
Repetitions: 6 per side.

Steps:

1. Step your left foot forward slightly.
2. Circle your left hand across your body as if brushing your knee.
3. Push your right hand forward gently.
4. Shift your weight forward.
5. Return to the center and switch sides.

Accessible Version:

The seated version uses the same arm pattern while sliding one foot forward slightly.

Before/After Notes:

Use this movement during practice to develop controlled, mindful stepping and coordinated movement. Afterward, allow your body to settle and notice a sense of steadiness and focus before moving on.

12. Parting the Wild Horse's Mane

Focus: Balance, coordination, and gentle whole-body movement.

Benefits:
This movement helps gently strengthen the legs, improve balance, and open the chest

for easier movement. It supports coordinated arm actions, encourages calm, rhythmic breathing, and promotes a relaxed, flowing sense of control.

Duration: 1 to 2 minutes.
Repetitions: 4 to 6 per side.

Steps:

1. Stand tall with your feet shoulder-width apart and knees softly bent.
2. Shift your weight gently onto your right foot.
3. Step your left foot slightly forward, keeping your stance comfortable.
4. As you shift your weight into the front foot, sweep your left hand forward as if offering or presenting something.
5. At the same time, your right hand moves down and back near your hip, creating a gentle opening through the chest.
6. Keep your shoulders relaxed and elbows soft.
7. Return to the center and repeat on the other side:
   - Step forward with your right foot.
   - Sweep the right hand forward.
   - Let the left hand relax and follow.

Accessible Version:
The seated version uses the same arm movements without stepping:

- Extend one hand forward while the opposite hand lowers.
- Switch sides slowly.
- Keep your feet grounded and your spine tall.

Before/After Notes:
Use this movement during practice, beginning with relaxed breathing and soft knees to support smooth, flowing motion. Afterward, gently roll your shoulders to release any remaining tension before continuing.

13. CIRCLE THE ARMS (HEAVEN AND EARTH MOTION)

Focus: Shoulder mobility and coordination.

Benefits:
This movement helps loosen stiff shoulders, improve flexibility, and encourage gentle,

circular movement through the arms. It promotes relaxation, supports coordinated motion, and helps restore a calm, centered feeling in the body.

Duration: 1 minute.
Repetitions: 8 circles upward, 8 downward.

Steps:

1. Stand or sit tall.
2. Lift your right hand upward in a circular arc.
3. Let it gently descend back down the same path.
4. Alternate arms.
5. Keep the movement slow and smooth.

Accessible Version:

The seated version is identical with smaller circles.

Before/After Notes:

Use this movement as a warm-up to prepare your shoulders and arms for upper-body movement. Afterward, let your arms rest comfortably and notice a feeling of openness and ease before continuing.

14. Turning the Waist

Focus: Spine flexibility and gentle rotation.

Benefits:
This movement helps reduce stiffness in the lower back and encourages gentle rotation through the waist. It supports healthy spine movement, improves ease of daily activities, and promotes greater comfort when turning.

Duration: 1 minute.
Repetitions: 10 turns per side.

Steps:

1. Stand or sit with your feet hip-width apart.
2. Let your arms hang loosely.
3. Slowly turn your torso to the left.
4. Allow your arms to swing gently.
5. Turn to the right.
6. Keep your breath calm and movements relaxed.

Accessible Version:
In the seated version, keep your feet grounded and rotate from the torso.

Before/After Notes:

Use this movement before or after longer routines to help reduce back tightness and ease into gentle rotation. Afterward, allow your torso to return to a neutral position and notice a greater sense of comfort and mobility.

CHAPTER 7: STRENGTH AND FLEXIBILITY

This chapter focuses on movements that build gentle strength and improve flexibility without strain. Each exercise helps your muscles support your joints, making everyday tasks such as standing up from a chair, bending to pick something up, or walking with confidence feel easier. These exercises also help loosen stiffness, which many seniors feel in the morning or after sitting for a long time.

You don't need force or speed here. Tai Chi strength comes from slow control, smooth motion, and mindful breathing. If you ever feel unsure, choose the seated version first. You can always move to the standing version later.

Remember, every exercise in this chapter is designed to help you feel stronger, steadier, and more comfortable in your own body.

Focus: Shoulder mobility and gentle upper-body strength.

Benefits:

This movement helps loosen the shoulders, improve posture, and encourage calm, steady breathing. It promotes relaxation in the upper body, supports body awareness, and helps create a light, relaxed feeling during movement.

Duration: 1 to 2 minutes.
Repetitions: 6 to 8 slow lifts.

Steps:

1. Stand or sit tall with your feet hip-width apart; keep your arms relaxed at your sides.
2. Inhale slowly as both hands rise in front of you to shoulder height, palms facing down.
3. Keep your shoulders soft and your elbows slightly bent.
4. Exhale as your hands float gently back down to your sides.

5. Move slowly, imagining your hands being lifted by air rather than muscle effort.
6. Continue this quiet lifting and lowering motion at a comfortable pace.

Accessible Version:

Sit with your back supported and your feet flat on the ground. Lift only to a height that feels natural and gentle for your shoulders.

Before/After Notes:

Use this movement at the beginning of a session to gently settle your body and prepare for flowing motion. Afterward, let your hands rest comfortably and take a slow, natural breath before continuing.

16. Lift and Lower the Heels

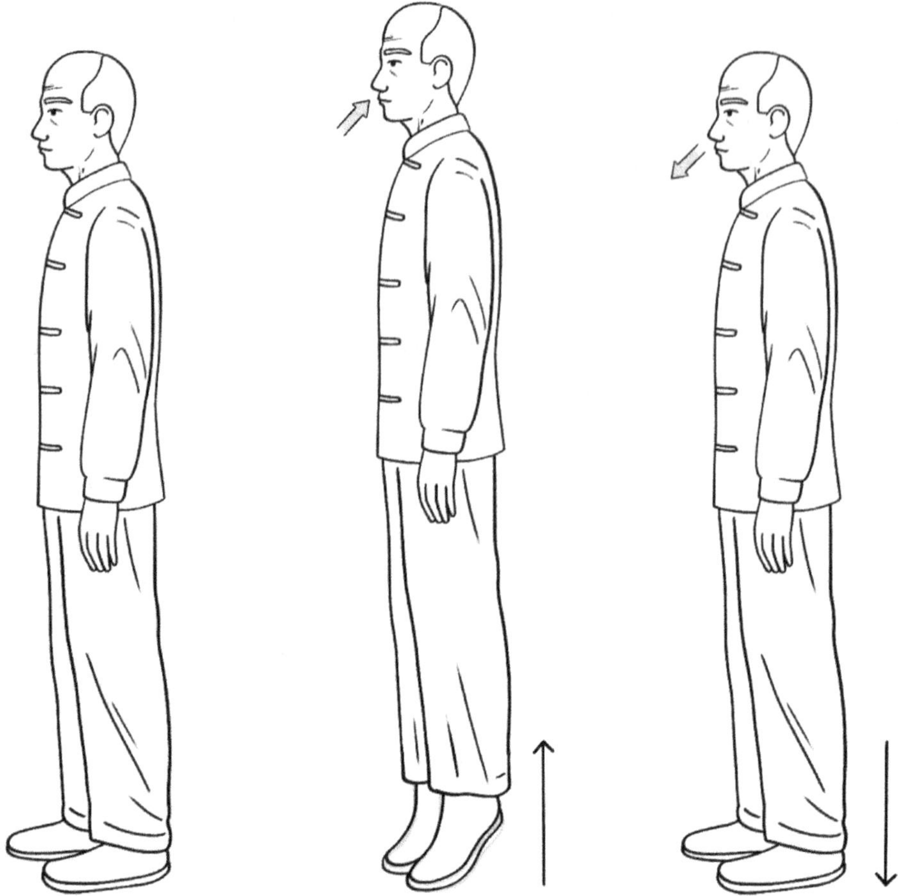

Focus: Ankle strength and lower-leg stability.

Benefits:
This movement helps improve balance, gently strengthen the calves, and support steady standing. It promotes safer, more confident walking and encourages better awareness of foot placement.

Duration: 1 to 2 minutes.
Repetitions: 10 to 12 heel lifts.

Steps:

1. Stand with your feet hip-width apart and hands resting lightly on the back of a chair for support, if needed.

2. Inhale as you slowly rise onto the balls of your feet.
3. Gently pause at the top without locking your knees.
4. Exhale as your heels lower back down with control.
5. Keep your posture tall and your shoulders relaxed throughout the movement.
6. Repeat steadily, allowing your ankles to warm and strengthen.

Accessible Version:
Sit tall with your feet flat on the ground. Lift both heels while keeping your toes on the floor, then lower slowly.

Before/After Notes:
Use this movement as a warm-up before balance exercises to gently prepare your legs and feet. Afterward, lightly shake out your legs, then pause to notice a sense of steadiness before moving on.

17. Seated Leg Extension

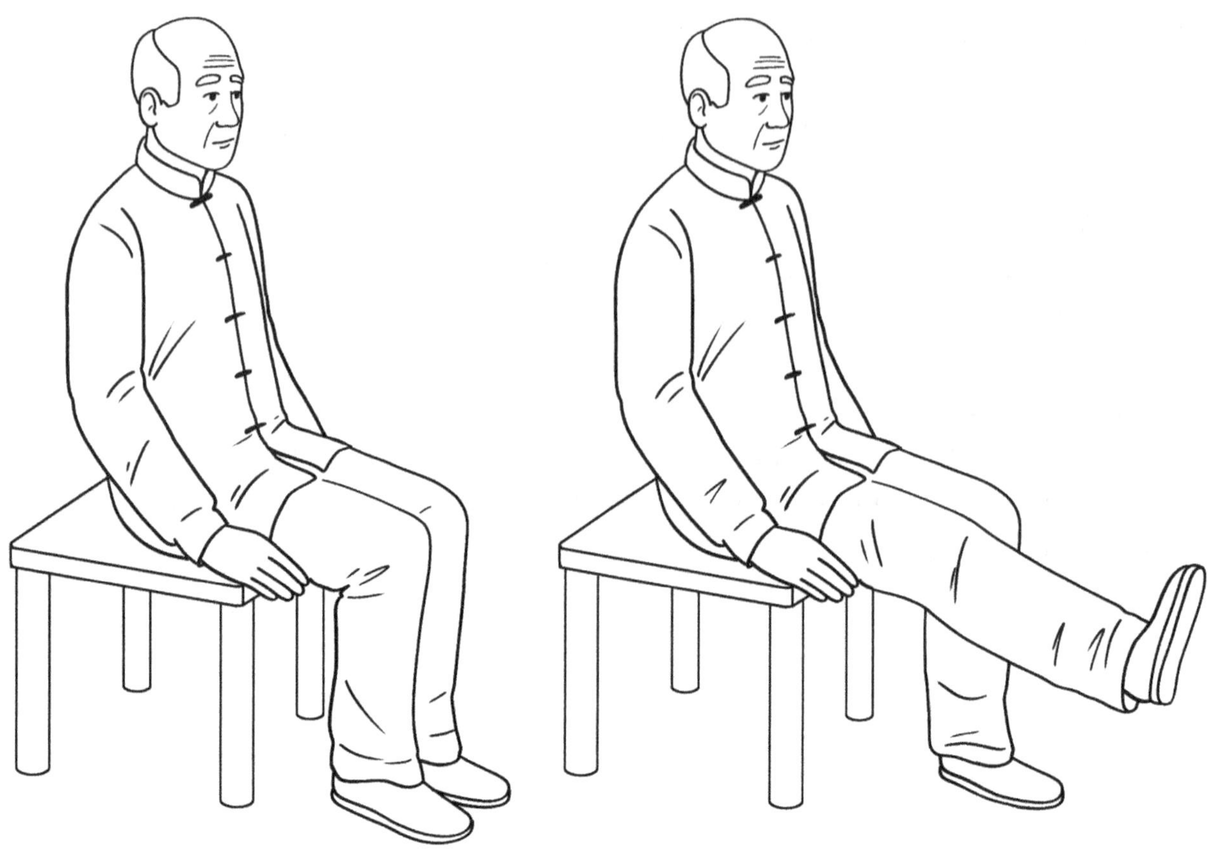

Focus: Knee strength and thigh activation.

Benefits:
This movement helps gently strengthen the thighs and support everyday actions such as standing and stair climbing. It encourages healthy circulation, improves leg awareness, and promotes confident, controlled movement while seated.

Duration: 1 minute.
Repetitions: 8 per leg.

Steps:

1. Sit near the front of a sturdy chair with your feet flat on the ground and your hands resting at your sides.
2. Inhale as you slowly extend your right leg forward until it is straight or nearly straight.

3. Gently flex your foot upward, feeling the thigh engage.
4. Exhale as your foot lowers back to the floor.
5. Repeat on the left side, moving slowly and evenly.
6. Keep your back upright and your shoulders relaxed.

Before/After Notes:
Use this movement during seated practice to gently strengthen your knees and legs. Afterward, if standing is comfortable, gently bend each knee once or twice and notice how your legs feel before continuing.

18. The Archer's Pull

Focus: Upper-back strength and chest opening.

Benefits:
This movement helps gently strengthen the back muscles, improve posture, and open the chest. It encourages focused, controlled movement, supports upper-body coordination, and promotes a calm, attentive state of mind.

Duration: 1 to 2 minutes.
Repetitions: 6 pulls per side.

Steps:

1. Stand or sit tall with your feet hip-width apart. Bring both hands to chest height as if holding a bow.
2. Inhale as the left hand extends forward like aiming an arrow.
3. At the same time, draw your right elbow back as if pulling a bowstring.
4. Keep your shoulders relaxed and eyes looking softly forward.
5. Exhale as both hands return to the center.
6. Repeat on the opposite side, alternating slowly and smoothly.

Accessible Version:

Perform the same motion while sitting, ensuring your elbows stay comfortable and movement is smaller.

Before/After Notes:

Use this movement during practice to support upright posture and balanced upper-body engagement. Afterward, gently roll your shoulders once and allow your body to return to a relaxed, neutral position.

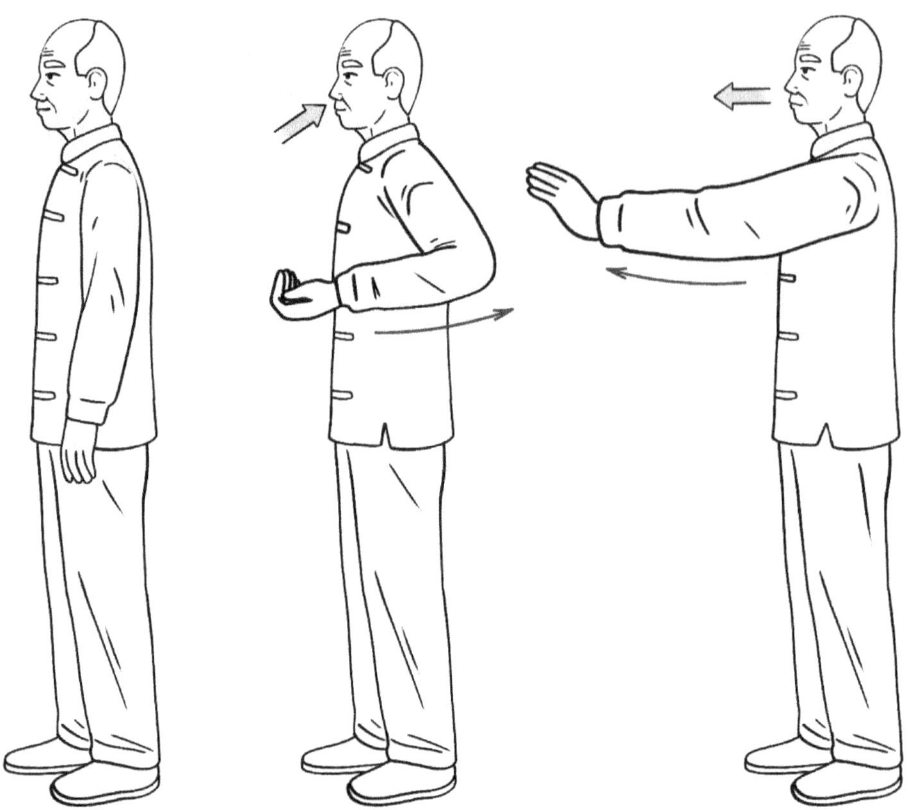

Focus: Core strength and gentle spinal movement.

Benefits:
This movement helps gently strengthen the back and core while encouraging smooth, coordinated movement. It supports controlled trunk rotation, improves body awareness, and promotes steady, comfortable motion.

Duration: 1 to 2 minutes.
Repetitions: 6 to 8 rows.

Steps:

1. Sit or stand comfortably with your legs shoulder-width apart and your arms extended slightly forward.
2. Inhale as you draw both elbows back, opening your chest as if rowing a paddle.

3. Keep your spine tall and shoulders soft.
4. Exhale as your hands extend forward again.
5. Move slowly, imagining gentle water resistance.
6. Continue the rowing motion, allowing your upper back to engage naturally.

Accessible Version:

While seated, follow the same steps but keep the movement smaller and avoid leaning too far forward or backward.

Before/After Notes:

Use this movement during practice to help loosen your back and encourage gentle trunk movement. Afterward, rest your hands on your thighs and take one calm, steady breath before continuing.

20. Push the Mountain

Focus: Arm strength and grounded stability.

Benefits:
This movement helps gently strengthen the arms, support leg stability, and encourage a grounded, steady stance. It promotes balance, builds confidence in standing, and supports calm, controlled movement.

Duration: 1 to 2 minutes.
Repetitions: 6 pushes.

Steps:

1. Stand or sit with your hands at chest height, palms facing outward.
2. Inhale as your elbows bend slightly toward your sides.
3. Exhale slowly as you press your hands forward as though pushing a mountain.

4. Keep your weight centered and posture upright.
5. Inhale as your hands return toward your chest.
6. Repeat slowly, imagining steady, controlled strength.

Accessible Version:
While seated, perform the same pushing motion, keeping your elbows close to avoid shoulder strain.

Before/After Notes:
Use this movement before balance exercises to help build stability and a grounded stance. Afterward, gently shake out your hands and allow your arms to relax before moving on.

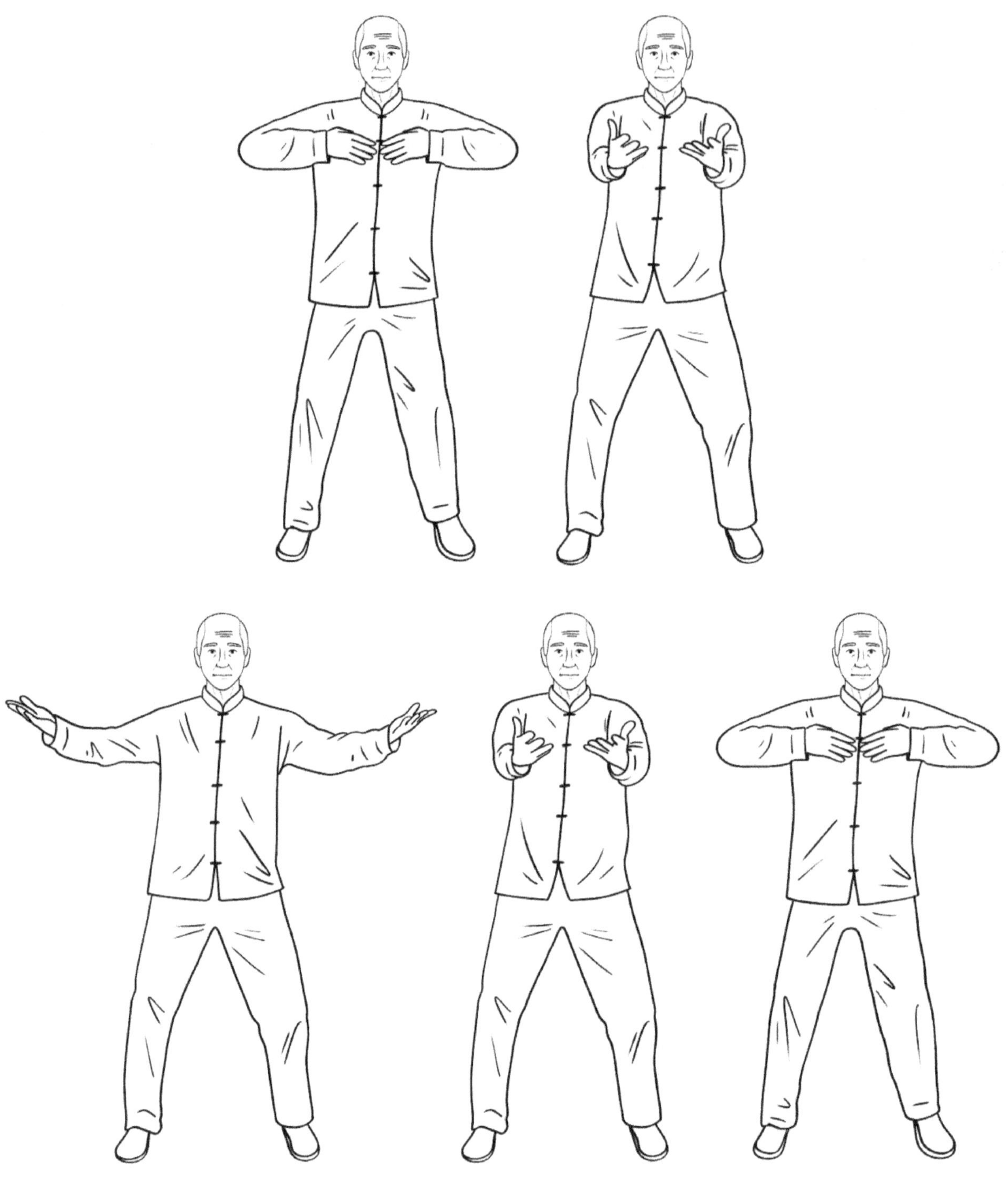

Focus: Chest expansion and arm flexibility.

Benefits:

This movement helps open the chest, loosen the arms, and encourage calm, steady breathing. It supports relaxed upper-body movement, improves posture, and promotes a sense of ease and openness.

Duration: 1 minute.
Repetitions: 6 to 8 openings.

Steps:

1. Sit or stand tall with your hands together at chest height, palms touching lightly.
2. Inhale as your hands slowly open outward like a flower blooming.
3. Keep your elbows soft as your chest expands.
4. Exhale as your hands return gently to the center.
5. Move slowly and smoothly, matching your breath.
6. Repeat at a relaxed pace.

Accessible Version:
Follow the steps while seated, but make the opening movement smaller if your shoulders feel tight.

Before/After Notes:
Use this movement during practice to support open posture and relaxed breathing. Afterward, place one hand on your chest and take a slow, gentle inhale before continuing.

CHAPTER 8: CALM AND BREATHING

This chapter is about slowing down and helping your body relax. The exercises focus on gentle breathing, smooth arm movements, and calm attention. They are especially helpful if you feel tense, anxious, tired, or overwhelmed. You can use this chapter on its own for relaxation, or add these movements at the end of a longer Tai Chi session.

There is no rush here. Move slowly, breathe comfortably, and rest whenever you need to. All exercises can be done seated or standing. Even a few minutes of calm breathing and gentle movement can help you feel steadier, clearer, and more at ease.

22. Holding the Ball (Qi Ball Breathing)

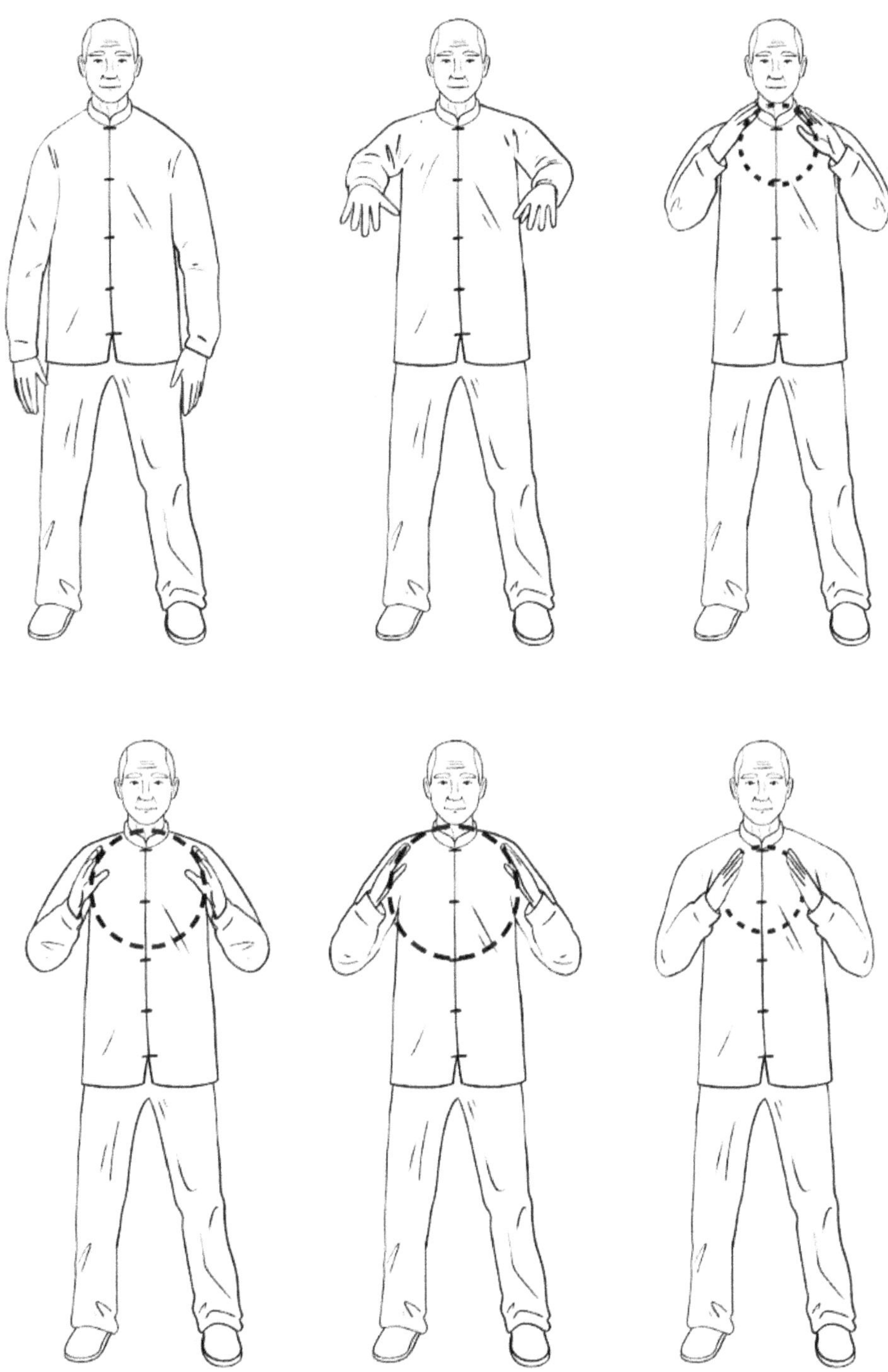

Focus: Breath awareness, relaxation, and gentle arm positioning.

Benefits:

This movement helps calm the nervous system, relax the shoulders, and encourage steady, mindful breathing. It improves breathing awareness, supports focused attention, and promotes a centered, relaxed feeling in the body.

Duration: 1 to 2 minutes.
Repetitions: 6 to 10 slow breaths.

Steps:

1. Stand or sit tall with your feet flat on the ground.
2. Raise your arms in front of your chest as if gently holding a large beach ball.
3. Keep your elbows rounded and relaxed, with your hands facing each other without touching.
4. Inhale slowly through your nose, imagining the ball expanding slightly.
5. Exhale gently through your mouth, allowing your shoulders to soften.
6. Keep your gaze relaxed and your breathing slow and steady.

Accessible Version:
Sit upright in a chair with your back supported if needed. Hold the imaginary ball closer to your chest if your shoulders tire.

Before/After Notes:
Use this movement during practice to settle your breath and focus attention inward. Before beginning, lightly shake out your arms to release tension, and after finishing, lower your hands to your lap and take one calm, steady breath.

23. FLOWING RIVER HANDS

Focus: Shoulder relaxation and smooth coordination.

Benefits:

This movement helps loosen the shoulders, calm the mind, and encourage smooth, steady breathing. It supports relaxed, flowing arm movement, enhances body awareness, and promotes a sense of ease and continuity.

Duration: 1 to 2 minutes.
Repetitions: 8 to 10 gentle flows.

Steps:

1. Stand or sit upright with your hands floating in front of your waist.
2. Inhale as both hands glide slowly to the left.
3. Exhale as your hands return through the center.
4. Inhale as your hands glide to the right.
5. Keep your movements smooth and continuous.
6. Imagine your hands moving like a calm river.

Accessible Version:
Perform the same motion seated, keeping your hands closer to your body.

Before/After Notes:
Use this movement during practice to help ease shoulder tension and encourage smooth, flowing arm movement. After finishing, gently roll your shoulders once or twice and notice a softer, more relaxed feeling before continuing.

24. Hands Like Clouds (Continuous Form)

Focus: Coordination, relaxation, and gentle waist movement.

Benefits:
This movement helps improve coordination, relax the upper body, and encourage smooth, continuous motion. It calms the mind, supports balanced movement, and promotes a steady, relaxed flow.

Duration: 2 minutes.
Repetitions: 4 to 6 slow passes per side.

Steps:

1. Stand or sit tall with your hands raised softly in front of your chest.
2. Move one hand upward while the other moves downward in a slow circle.
3. Shift slightly to the left as your hands circle.
4. Reverse the hand positions as you shift to the right.
5. Keep your movements smooth and flowing.
6. Breathe naturally throughout.

Accessible Version:

Remain seated and focus only on the arm circles without shifting side to side.

Before/After Notes:

Use this movement during practice to calm your mind and encourage smooth, continuous motion. After finishing, pause quietly for one natural breath and notice a sense of ease before continuing.

25. Drawing Down the Sky

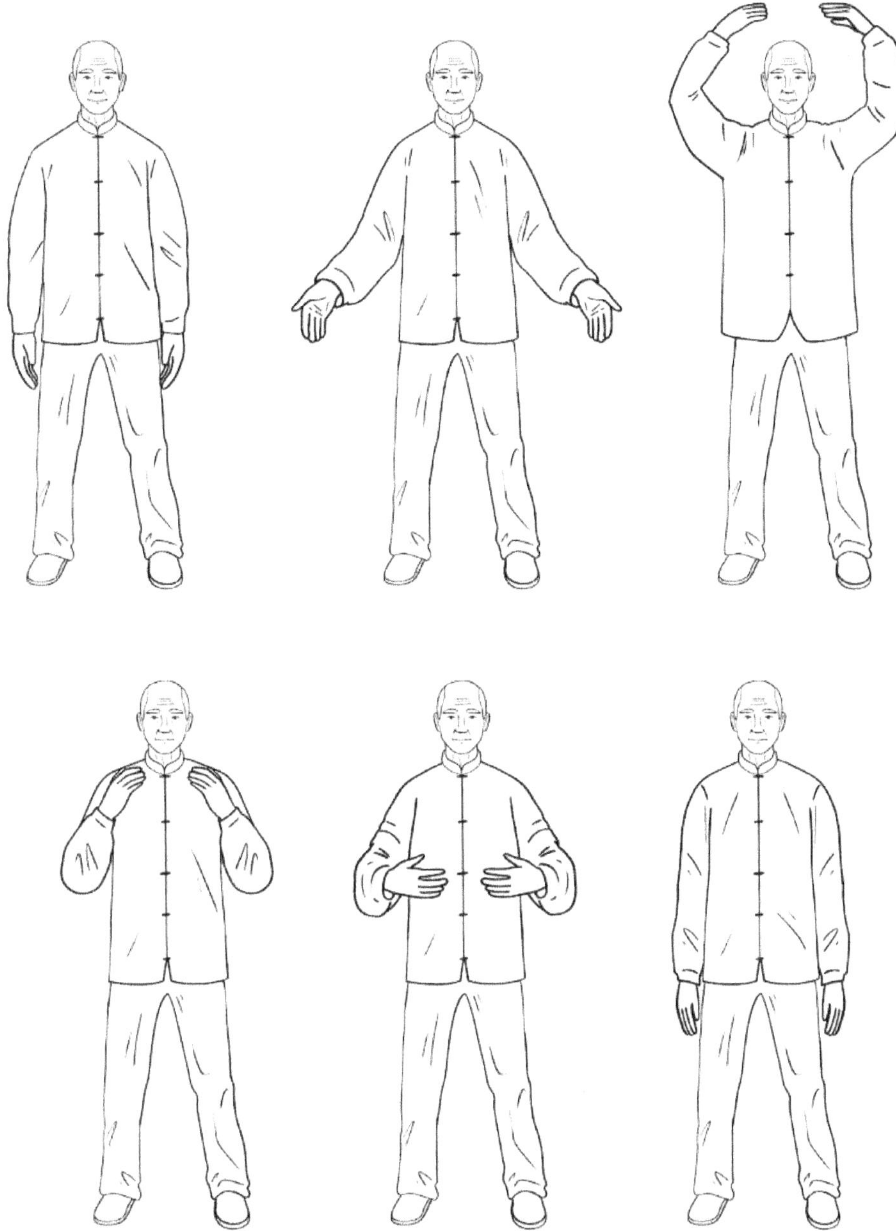

Focus: Breath coordination and full-body relaxation.

Benefits:

This movement helps calm the nervous system, encourage deeper breathing, and relax the shoulders. It supports gentle upper-body release, improves breathing awareness, and promotes a sense of calm and balance.

Duration: 1 to 2 minutes.

Repetitions: 6 slow draws.

Steps:

1. Stand or sit tall with your arms relaxed at your sides.
2. Inhale as both hands rise gently overhead, palms facing upward.
3. Exhale slowly as your hands float down in front of your body.
4. Keep the movement slow and controlled.
5. Avoid lifting your arms too high if your shoulders feel tight.
6. Repeat at a calm pace.

Accessible Version:

If practicing seated, lift the arms only to a comfortable height, stopping around shoulder level if needed.

Before/After Notes:

Use this movement near the end of a session to help your body settle and prepare for rest. After finishing, sit quietly for one slow, comfortable breath before moving on.

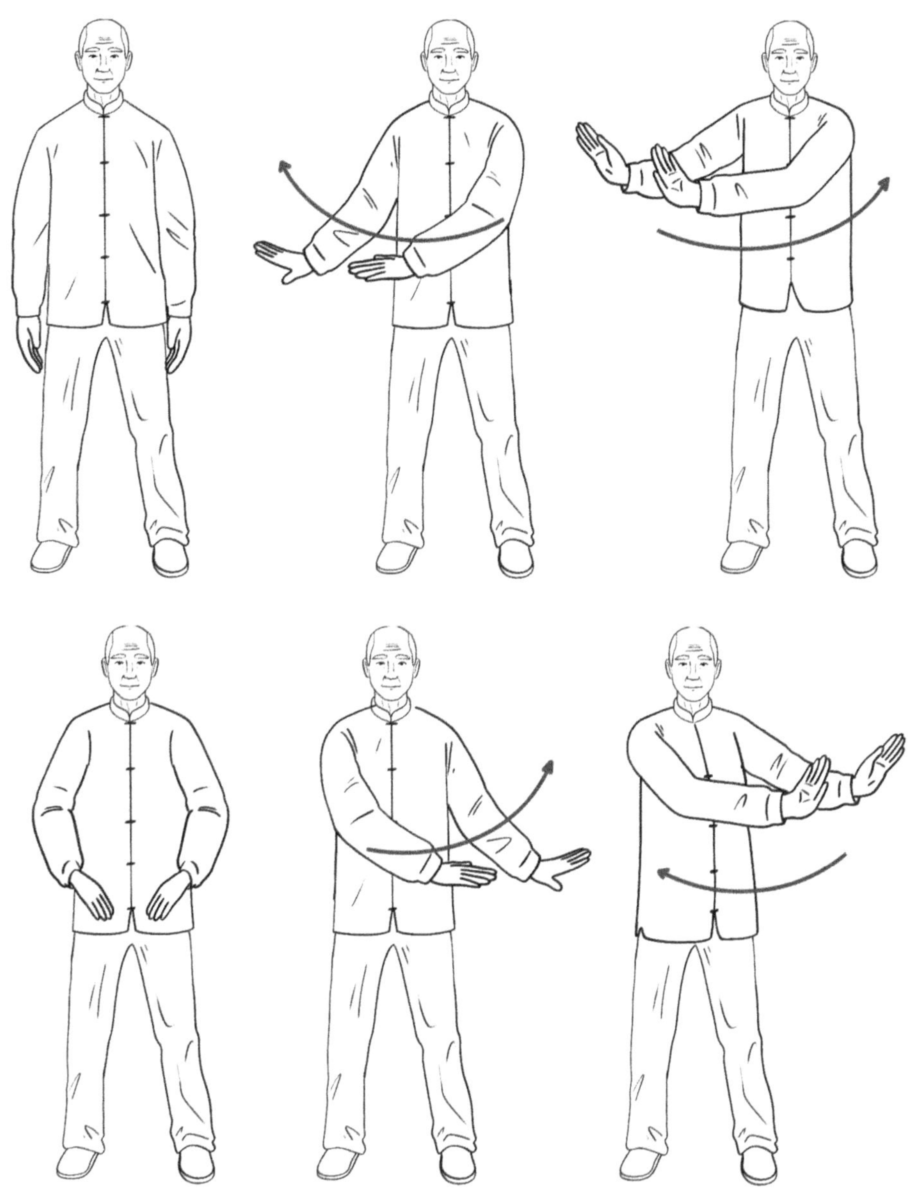

Focus: Relaxation and breath rhythm.

Benefits:
This movement helps reduce stress, soften muscle tension, and encourage slow, controlled breathing. It improves breath awareness, promotes relaxation throughout the body, and supports a calm, steady rhythm.

Duration: 1 to 2 minutes.

Repetitions: 6 to 8 wave motions.

Steps:

1. Stand or sit comfortably with your feet flat on the ground and your hands resting near your waist.
2. Inhale as your hands rise in a gentle wave motion toward the right side.
3. As your hands move right, let your torso softly turn to the left, keeping your shoulders relaxed.
4. Exhale as your hands lower slowly back toward the center, like waves returning to the shore.
5. Inhale again as your hands rise toward the left side.
6. As your hands move left, allow your torso to gently turn to the right.
7. Let your breath guide the rhythm of the movement.
8. Keep your face relaxed, jaw soft, and movements smooth.
9. Continue at an easy, flowing pace.

Accessible Version:
While seated, follow the same steps but make smaller wave motions.

Before/After Notes:
Use this movement during practice to calm your body and settle your breath. Afterward, place one hand on your belly and breathe slowly, noticing a steady, soothing rhythm.

27. CLOSE THE CIRCLE

Focus: Grounding and completion.

Benefits:
This movement helps ground the body, calm the mind, and gently bring the practice to a close. It supports relaxation, encourages a sense of completion, and helps the body settle into a balanced, restful state.

Duration: 1 minute.
Repetitions: 3 slow circles.

Steps:

1. Stand or sit upright with your hands at torso height, palms facing inward.
2. Inhale as your hands trace an outward circle.
3. Exhale as your hands return gently toward your chest and then in front of your torso.
4. Keep the movements slow and controlled.
5. Focus on steady breathing.
6. Repeat calmly.

Accessible Version:
Perform the same movement while seated with relaxed arms.

Before/After Notes:
Use this movement as the final part of a routine to gently bring the practice to a close. Afterward, pause quietly and notice a sense of calm and completion before resting.

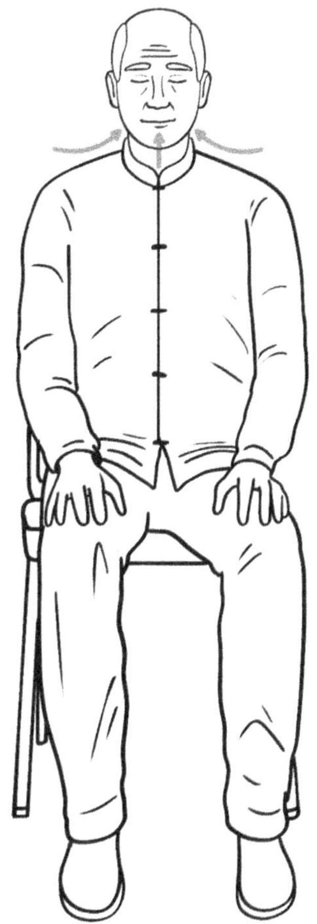 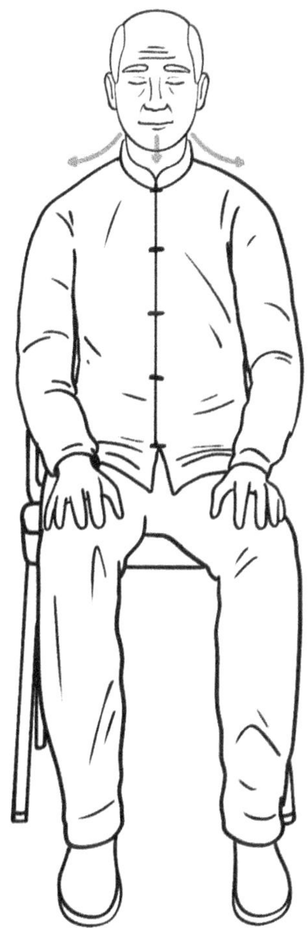

Focus: Breath awareness and relaxation.

Benefits:
This movement helps reduce feelings of anxiety, improve focus, and encourage deep relaxation. It supports steady breathing, promotes mental calm, and helps the body feel settled and at ease while seated.

Duration: 2 minutes.
Repetitions: 6 to 10 slow breaths.

Steps:

1. Sit comfortably with your feet flat on the ground.
2. Place your hands on your thighs or belly.

3. Inhale gently through your nose.
4. Exhale slowly through your mouth.
5. Let your shoulders drop with each breath.
6. Continue breathing calmly.

Accessible Version:
This exercise is already fully seated and accessible.

Before/After Notes:
Use this movement at any point in a session when you feel tense or unsettled to encourage calm and steady breathing. After finishing, open your eyes slowly and notice a sense of ease before continuing or resting.

CHAPTER 9: JOINT RELIEF AND ACCESSIBILITY

This chapter is designed to help you move with less discomfort and more confidence, especially on days when your joints feel stiff, sore, or tired. Many seniors experience tightness in the neck, shoulders, hips, knees, and hands from daily activities or long periods of sitting. The exercises in this chapter focus on gentle joint movement, circulation, and ease rather than effort.

Every exercise can be done seated or with support. There is no need to push through pain or discomfort. Small, slow movements are enough to keep your joints healthy and flexible. These exercises are especially helpful in the morning, before bed, or on rest days when you still want to move but need something lighter.

You may choose just one or two exercises, or move through the whole chapter at your own pace. Listen to your body and rest whenever needed. When done regularly, gentle movement helps maintain independence and comfort over time.

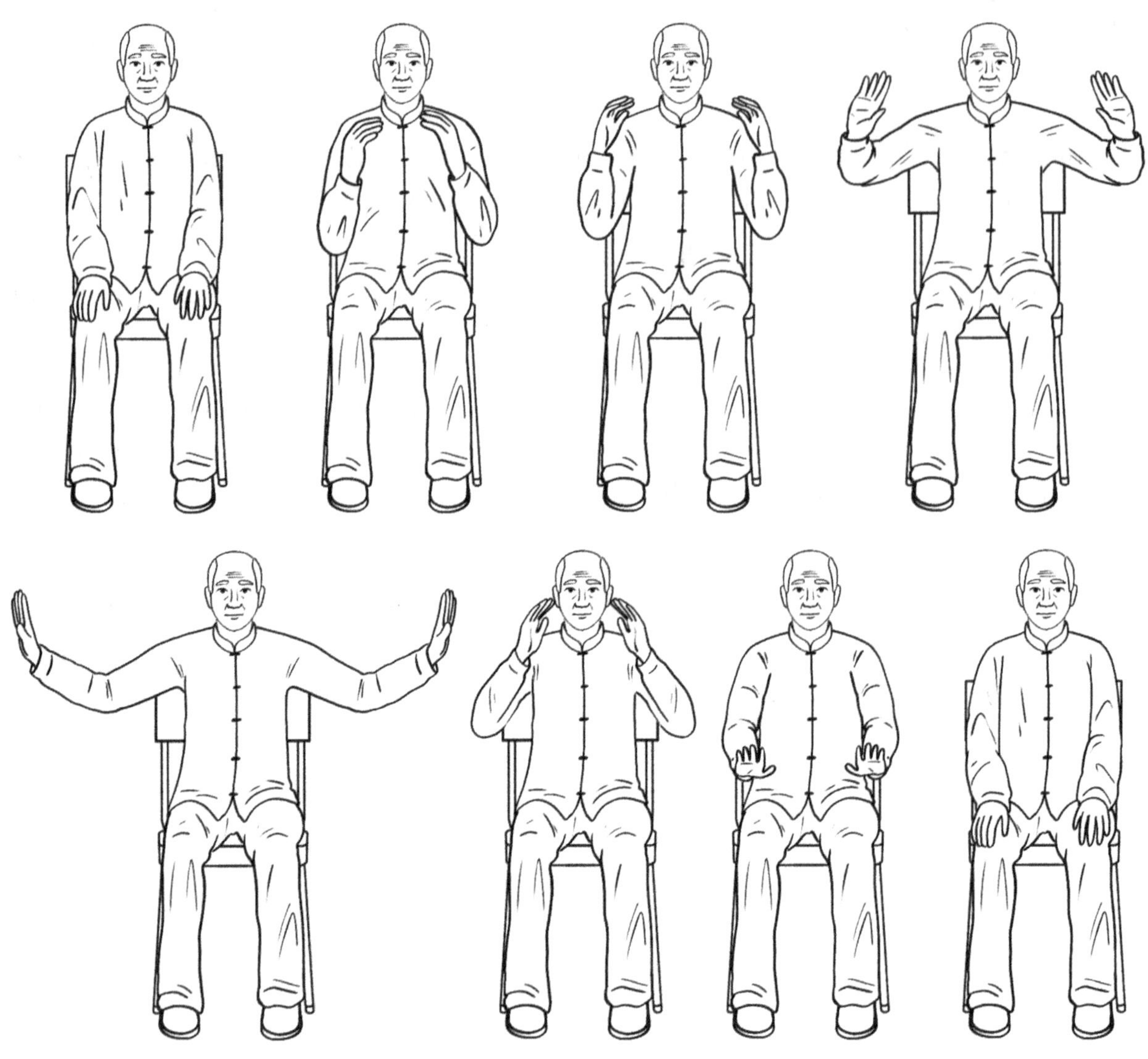

Focus: Shoulder mobility, circulation, and gentle coordination.

Benefits:

This movement helps loosen the shoulders, reduce arm stiffness, and encourage gentle circulation through the arms. It promotes relaxed, flowing movement, supports body awareness, and encourages a calm, comfortable feeling while seated.

Duration: 1 to 2 minutes.
Repetitions: 6 to 8 slow cycles.

Steps:

1. Sit tall in a chair with both feet flat on the ground.
2. Rest your hands on your thighs with your palms facing down.
3. Inhale as you slowly lift both arms forward and upward to chest height.
4. Turn your palms outward and gently open your arms to the sides.
5. Exhale as you lower your arms back down, returning to the center, then returning your hands to your thighs.
6. Keep the movements smooth and unhurried.
7. Let your breath guide the flow of your arms.

Accessible Version:

This exercise is already fully seated. If needed, lift your arms only partway.

Before/After Notes:

Use this movement during seated practice to encourage relaxed, flowing arm movement. Before starting, allow your shoulders to soften, and after finishing, rest your hands on your lap and take one calm, steady breath.

30. Gentle Neck Turns

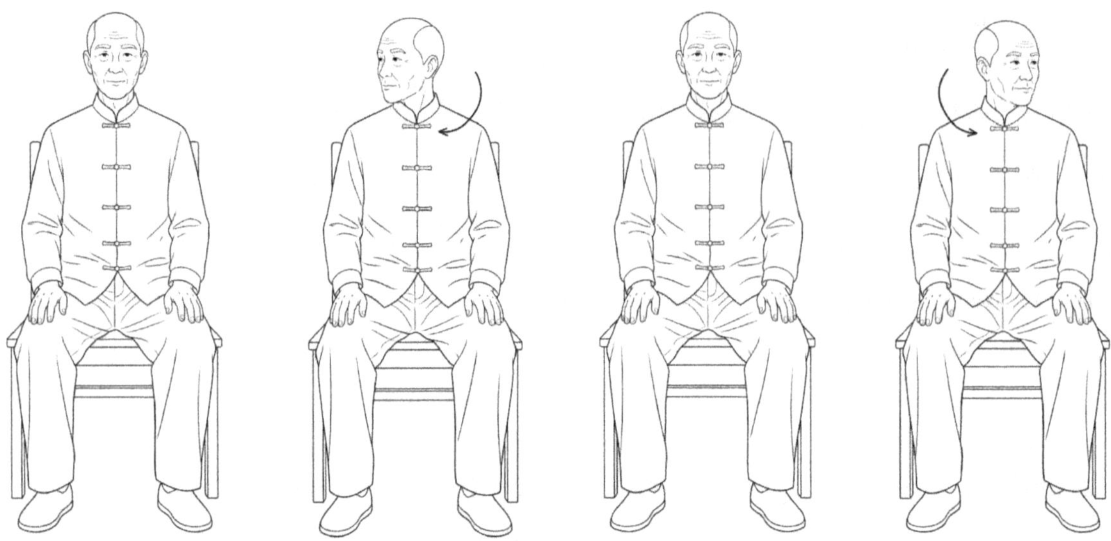

Focus: Neck mobility and tension relief.

Benefits:
This movement helps reduce neck stiffness, ease built-up tension, and encourage gentle head movement. It improves neck mobility, supports everyday comfort, and promotes relaxed awareness through the upper body.

Duration: 1 minute.
Repetitions: 6 turns per side.

Steps:

1. Sit or stand upright with your shoulders relaxed.
2. Look straight ahead and take a slow breath.
3. Gently turn your head to the right, stopping before discomfort.
4. Pause briefly, then return to the center.
5. Turn your head slowly to the left.
6. Keep the movements small and controlled.
7. Continue alternating sides at an easy pace.

Accessible Version:
Remain seated with your back supported. Make the movements very small if needed.

Before/After Notes:
Use this movement during practice to ease tension through your neck and upper shoulders. Before starting, allow your shoulders to drop and relax, and after finishing, return your head to the center and breathe slowly before continuing.

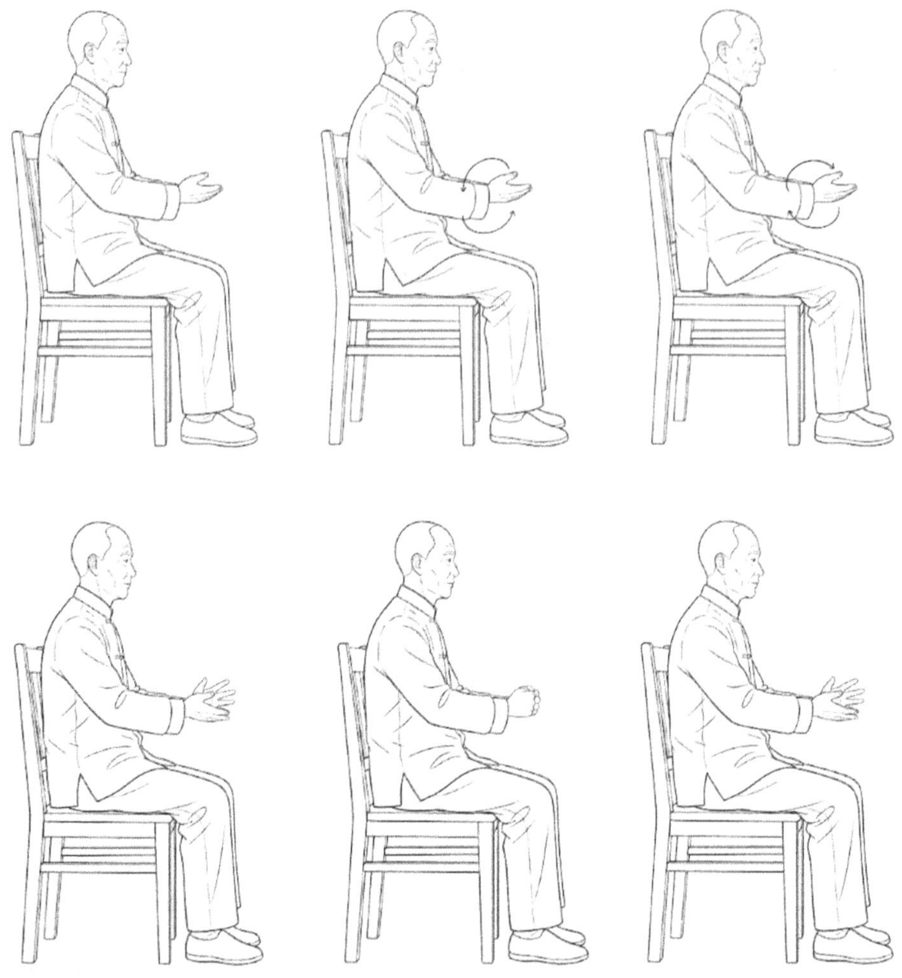

Focus: Hand mobility and joint lubrication.

Benefits:
This movement helps improve wrist flexibility, reduce hand stiffness, and encourage gentle movement through the hands and fingers. It supports comfortable daily hand use, enhances circulation, and promotes relaxed coordination.

Duration: 1 to 2 minutes.
Repetitions: 6 to 10 circles in each direction.

Steps:

1. Sit comfortably with your elbows bent and your hands in front of you.

2. Slowly rotate both wrists in small circles.
3. Reverse direction after several rotations.
4. Gently open your fingers wide.
5. Slowly close your hands into a loose fist.
6. Move without force or strain.

Accessible Version:
Rest your forearms on the chair's armrests or on your thighs if your arms feel tired.

Before/After Notes:
Use this movement during practice to gently warm and mobilize the wrists and fingers. Before starting, lightly shake out your hands, and after finishing, rest them comfortably on your thighs and notice a sense of ease.

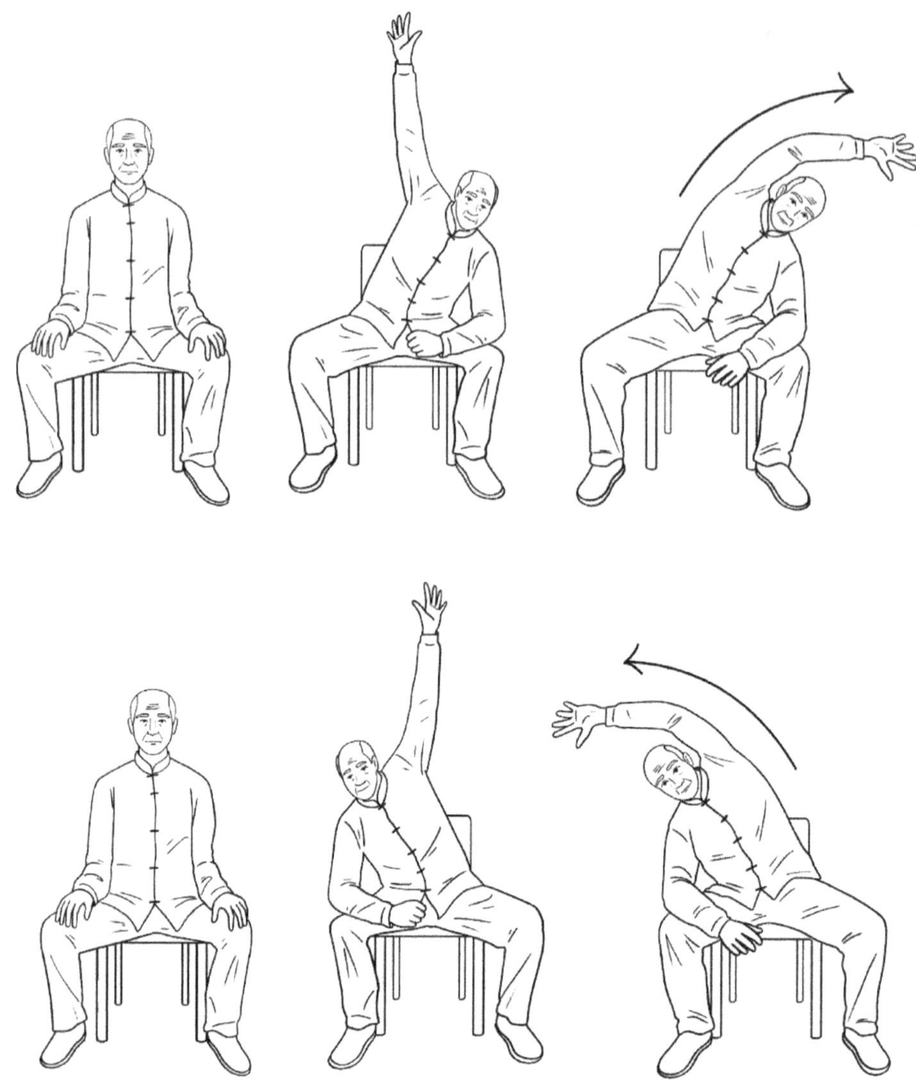

Focus: Side body flexibility and spine mobility.

Benefits:
This movement helps gently stretch the sides of the body, ease back tension, and encourage comfortable spinal movement. It improves flexibility through the spine, supports upright posture, and promotes a feeling of space and ease while seated.

Duration: 1 to 2 minutes.
Repetitions: 4 to 6 bends per side.

Steps:

1. Sit tall in a chair with your feet placed wide apart and flat on the ground.
2. Rest your left elbow gently on your left thigh for support.
3. Inhale as you slowly raise your right arm overhead.
4. As you exhale, gently bend your torso to the left, reaching your right hand over your head.
5. Keep your chest open and avoid twisting the shoulders.
6. Hold the stretch briefly while breathing comfortably.
7. Inhale as you return slowly to the center.
8. Lower your arm and repeat on the opposite side.

Accessible Version:

If raising the arm overhead is uncomfortable, lift it only partway or rest the raised hand near the side of your head.

Before/After Notes:

Use this movement during seated practice to encourage gentle side stretching and comfort through your spine. Before starting, sit upright with your shoulders relaxed, and after finishing, rest both hands on your thighs and take one slow, natural breath before continuing.

33. Hip Circles (Standing or Seated)

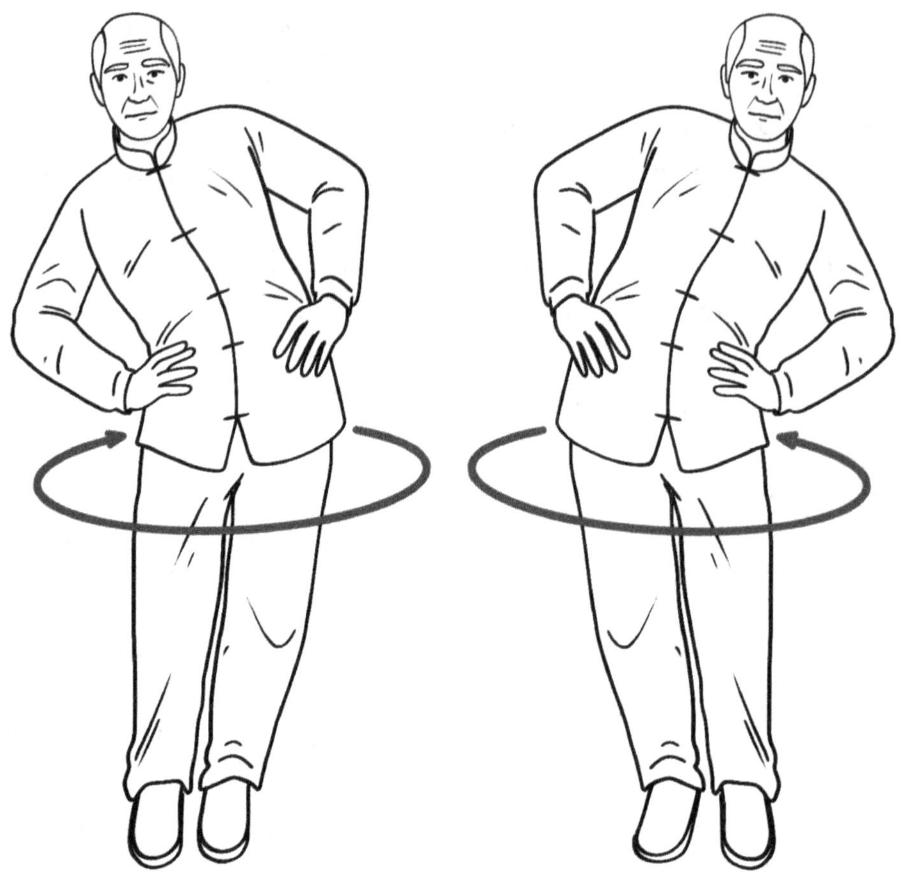

Focus: Hip mobility and lower body comfort.

Benefits:
This movement helps improve hip flexibility, reduce stiffness, and encourage smooth, comfortable movement through the hips. It supports easier walking, enhances balance, and promotes greater ease during everyday activities.

Duration: 1 to 2 minutes.
Repetitions: 6 circles in each direction.

Steps:

1. Stand with your hands on your hips or sit tall in a chair.
2. Slowly shift your hips forward in a small circle.
3. Continue the circle to the side, back, and around.

4. Reverse direction after several circles.
5. Keep the movements slow and controlled.

Accessible Version:
Perform the move fully seated with smaller movements.

Before/After Notes:
Use this movement during practice to encourage a comfortable, circular motion through your hips. Before starting, make sure you feel stable and supported, and after finishing, sit or stand quietly for a moment and notice a sense of ease before continuing.

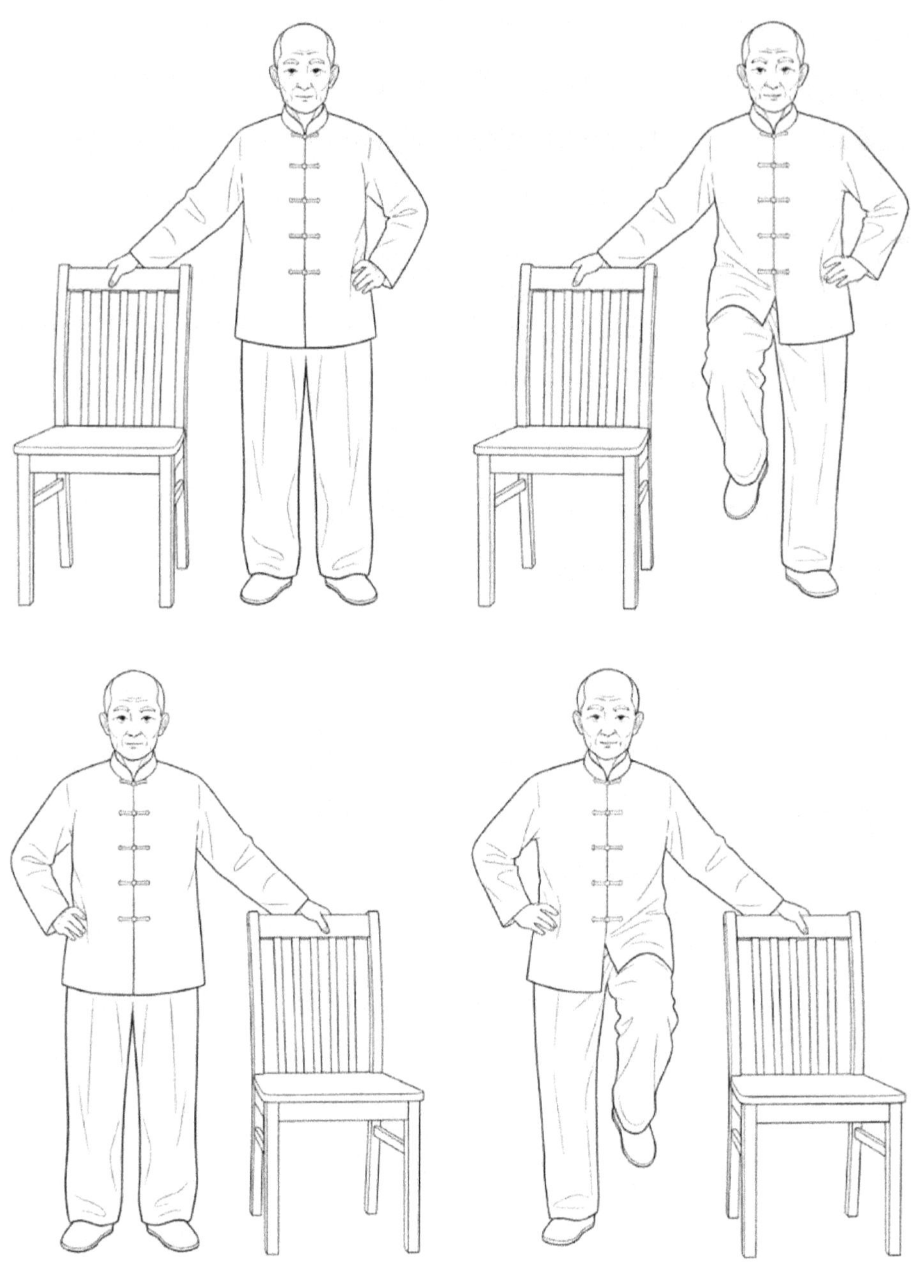

Focus: Knee mobility and leg strength.

Benefits:

This movement helps to gently strengthen the legs, support comfortable knee movement, and encourage balance awareness. It builds confidence when lifting the feet, supports steady standing, and promotes safer, controlled movement.

Duration: 1 to 2 minutes.
Repetitions: 6 to 8 lifts per leg.

Steps:

1. Stand holding a chair or sit upright.
2. Lift your right knee slowly.
3. Lower your right foot gently back down.
4. Switch to the left leg.
5. Keep the movements controlled and steady.

Accessible Version:
Perform the move seated, lifting one knee at a time.

Before/After Notes:
Use this movement during practice to support controlled leg lifting and balance awareness. Before starting, make sure your support is secure, and after finishing, place both feet comfortably on the floor and pause briefly before continuing.

Focus: Side body flexibility and spine comfort.

Benefits:
This movement helps gently improve flexibility along the sides of the body and ease back tension. It supports upright posture, encourages comfortable spinal movement, and promotes a sense of openness and ease.

Duration: 1 minute.
Repetitions: 4 to 6 stretches per side.

Steps:

1. Sit or stand tall with your arms relaxed.
2. Raise both arms gently overhead.
3. Lean slightly to the left without forcing.
4. Return to the center.
5. Repeat on the other side.

Accessible Version:

Perform the move seated; keep your arm lower or perform with your hands on your thighs.

Before/After Notes:

Use this movement during practice to encourage gentle stretching along the sides of your body. Before starting, sit upright with your shoulders relaxed, and after finishing, let your arms relax and return to calm, steady breathing.

Part 3: The 28-Day Gentle Tai Chi Challenge

This part of the book brings everything together into a gentle 28-day Tai Chi challenge, helping you build a steady habit one day at a time. Each day's practice takes about ten minutes and is designed to feel manageable and safe.

The challenge is not about pushing yourself or doing everything perfectly; it's about showing up, moving slowly, and giving your body regular care. You will repeat familiar exercises from earlier chapters, growing more comfortable and confident as the days go on.

Each week has a clear focus, such as posture, balance, strength, flow, or calm. The routines are short and predictable. You can follow the plan as written or adjust it to match how your body feels.

Helpful tips on pacing yourself, staying motivated, and listening to your body are included throughout. Some days will feel easier than others, and that is completely normal. What matters most is consistency.

Use this challenge as a gentle companion. Move at your own pace and breathe comfortably. Even a few minutes a day can help you feel steadier and calmer.

CHAPTER 10: HOW TO FOLLOW THE CHALLENGE

This 28-day Gentle Tai Chi Challenge is designed to fit comfortably into your daily life. You don't need to change your schedule, push your body, or aim for perfection. The goal is simple and achievable: move gently for about ten minutes a day, most days of the week, and allow steady progress to happen naturally.

How the Challenge Works (Ten Minutes a Day for Twenty-Eight Days)

Each day of the challenge includes a short Tai Chi routine made up of exercises you have already learned in Part Two. Most days will feel familiar, with small changes that help your body gradually build strength, balance, flexibility, and calm. Some days may feel easier than others, and that is completely normal.

Ten minutes may not sound like much, but when done consistently, gentle movement is powerful. Over time, these short daily sessions will help you feel steadier on your feet, looser in your joints, and more confident in your body.

You are encouraged to move at your own pace. If a routine takes a little longer, that's perfectly fine. If you need to stop early, that's also fine. The goal of this challenge is to support you, not to pressure you.

Tips for Staying Consistent and Motivated

Consistency matters more than intensity. Try linking your practice to something you already do each day, such as after waking up, before lunch, or in the early evening. Keeping your Tai Chi time consistent makes it easier to remember and easier to enjoy.

Some days you may feel motivated and energized, while on other days you may feel tired or distracted. On those days, remind yourself that even a few minutes of gentle movement is enough. Showing up is the win.

You may also find it helpful to keep a simple note of how you feel after each session. Many people notice they feel calmer, lighter, or more relaxed afterward, and this can be motivating in itself.

Your body is your best guide. Tai Chi should never cause pain. Mild stretching or gentle muscle effort is fine, but sharp pain or discomfort is a sign to stop or adjust the movement.

You are always free to choose the seated version of any exercise, reduce the range of motion, or take a rest day when needed. The challenge is flexible by design, and progress comes from listening, not pushing.

Trust that steady, gentle effort is enough. You are building strength and balance in a way that respects your body and supports long-term health.

CHAPTER 11: YOUR 28-DAY PLAN OVERVIEW

This chapter gives you a clear picture of how the 28-day challenge is structured and how to use it in a way that feels calm, organized, and manageable. You don't need to read everything at once; you can return to this chapter whenever you want a reminder of how the plan works.

How to Use the Weekly Routine Format

The challenge is organized into four weeks, each with a gentle focus. Every week includes a group of exercises drawn from the *Tai Chi Exercise Library* in Part Two. Repeat these exercises throughout the week so your body can become familiar with them.

Repetition is intentional. Doing the same movements several times allows you to feel more confident and relaxed with each session. You may notice that movements feel smoother or easier as the days go by.

You can follow the routines exactly as written or you can make small adjustments. If an exercise feels especially helpful, you can stay with it a little longer. If something feels difficult, you can shorten it or simply skip it.

Suggested Schedule and Practice Time

Choose a time of day when you are least rushed. Many seniors enjoy practicing in the morning to loosen stiff joints or in the late afternoon to unwind. There is no "best" time, only what works best for you.

Try to practice in the same general time window each day. This builds a gentle habit and reduces decision-making. However, if you miss a day, simply show up the next day without guilt or pressure.

You don't need special clothing; comfortable clothes that allow for easy movement are enough.

BREATHING AND REFLECTION BETWEEN MOVEMENTS

Make sure to take one or two slow breaths in between exercises. This short pause will help your body settle and prepare you for the next movement. Remember, Tai Chi is not meant to feel rushed.

You can also take a brief moment at the end of each session to notice how you feel. Some people feel calmer, while others feel warmer or more relaxed. There is no right or wrong experience.

WHAT YOU'LL NEED (JUST A CHAIR AND SOME SPACE)

All you need is a sturdy chair and a small, clear space. You can practice in your living room, bedroom, or any quiet area. Standing exercises can always be done near a wall or chair for support.

No equipment, mats, or special tools are required.

CHAPTER 12: WEEK 1 - GENTLE AWARENESS (DAYS 1-7)

Welcome to your first week of the Gentle Tai Chi Challenge. This week is about awareness rather than effort. There is no rush, no pressure, and no need to perform the movements perfectly. Your only task is to move slowly and notice how your body and breath feel.

During Week One, you will focus on posture, breathing, and balance; these are the foundations of Tai Chi and of everyday movement. Simple actions such as standing up, reaching forward, or shifting your weight all become easier when posture and breath are steady.

Each day, you will practice the same short routine for about ten minutes. Repeating the same movements helps your body feel safe and familiar with the practice. You don't need to memorize anything or push yourself to do more. Slow, comfortable movement is exactly what Tai Chi is meant to be.

If at any point you feel tired or uncomfortable, it's perfectly fine to sit down, pause, or stop early. Listening to your body is part of the practice, not a setback.

At the end of each session, take a quiet moment to notice how you feel. You don't need to analyze or judge anything; simply observe your shoulders, your breathing, and your overall sense of ease. Over time, these small moments of awareness will produce meaningful change.

Daily Routine (10 Minutes):

- **Centering Breath** | *Exercise 1, Chapter 5: Foundation and Posture (p. 16)*
- **Mountain Stance** | *Exercise 2, Chapter 5: Foundation and Posture (p. 18)*
- **Shoulder Roll Release** | *Exercise 4, Chapter 5: Foundation and Posture (p. 22)*
- **Open the Chest and Breathe** | *Exercise 5, Chapter 5: Foundation and Posture (p. 24)*
- **Gentle Weight Shift** | *Exercise 6, Chapter 5: Foundation and Posture (p. 26)*
- **Close the Circle** | *Exercise 27, Chapter 8: Calm and Breathing (p. 71)*

REFLECTION:

After finishing today's practice, pause for a few seconds. Notice whether your shoulders feel lighter or more relaxed. Pay attention to your breathing; does it feel slower or easier than when you began? Simply observe without trying to change anything.

CHAPTER 13: WEEK 2 – BUILDING STRENGTH AND STABILITY (DAYS 8-14)

In Week Two, you will begin to gently build strength and stability, especially in your legs and posture. This doesn't mean pushing harder or straining your body. Instead, it means learning how to feel supported and grounded as you move.

The exercises this week will help your legs feel steadier and your movements more confident. These skills support daily activities, such as standing for longer periods, stepping forward, or feeling secure when changing direction. You may notice mild muscle effort, which is normal, as long as it feels comfortable and controlled.

You will continue practicing for about ten minutes each day using the same routine throughout the week. Familiar movements allow your body to adapt gradually. If a movement feels challenging, use the seated version or reduce the repetitions. Remember, strength grows through consistent practice, not force.

This week is also about confidence. As your body becomes more familiar with these movements, you will notice that you trust your balance a little more. That trust will carry into everyday life.

At the end of each session, take a moment to notice any small changes. Strength often shows up quietly as a feeling of steadiness rather than something dramatic.

DAILY ROUTINE (10 MINUTES):

- **Centering Breath** | *Exercise 1, Chapter 5: Foundation and Posture (p. 16)*
- **Root Like a Tree** | *Exercise 7, Chapter 5: Foundation and Posture (p. 28)*
- **Brush Knee and Push** | *Exercise 11, Chapter 6: Balance and Coordination (p. 37)*
- **Lift and Lower the Heels** | *Exercise 16, Chapter 7: Strength and Flexibility (p. 48)*
- **The Archer's Pull** | *Exercise 18, Chapter 7: Strength and Flexibility (p. 52)*
- **Seated Leg Extension** | *Exercise 17, Chapter 7: Strength and Flexibility (p. 50)*

REFLECTION:

When your practice is complete, notice how your legs and posture feel. Do you feel more grounded or steady, even slightly? Take a calm breath and acknowledge the effort you made today, regardless of how strong or tired you feel.

CHAPTER 14: WEEK 3 - FLOW AND COORDINATION (DAYS 15-21)

By Week Three, you will have learned the basics of posture, balance, and gentle strength. This week focuses on flow and coordination, helping your movements feel smoother and more connected.

In Tai Chi, flow means moving from one motion to the next without rushing or tension. It's not about making the movements look perfect. It's about allowing your body to move naturally, guided by slow breathing and gentle attention.

The exercises this week invite your arms, legs, and torso to work together. This kind of coordination supports everyday movements like turning, reaching, or walking with ease. If you feel unsure at any point, slow down or return to a seated option.

Continue practicing for about ten minutes each day. Allow each movement to finish before starting the next. If your mind wanders, gently bring your attention back to your breath and the motion of your body.

Many people find this week especially calming. Repeating flowing movements can help quiet the mind and reduce tension.

Daily Routine (10 Minutes):

- **Open the Chest** | *Exercise 5, Chapter 5: Foundation and Posture (p. 24)*
- **Wave the Hands Like Water** | *Exercise 9, Chapter 6: Balance and Coordination (p. 33)*
- **Row the Boat** | *Exercise 19, Chapter 7: Strength and Flexibility (p. 54)*
- **Hands Like Clouds** | *Exercise 24, Chapter 8: Calm and Breathing (p. 65)*
- **Push the Mountain** | *Exercise 20, Chapter 7: Strength and Flexibility (p. 56)*
- **Drawing Down the Sky** | *Exercise 25, Chapter 8: Calm and Breathing (p. 67)*

After today's practice, notice the quality of your movement. Did your motions feel smoother or more relaxed than before? Even if only for a moment, acknowledge any sense of rhythm or ease you experienced.

CHAPTER 15: WEEK 4 – CALM AND RENEWAL (DAYS 22-28)

Your final week is about calm, renewal, and carrying the Tai Chi mindset into daily life. By now, the movements should feel familiar, allowing you to focus more on how they feel rather than how they look.

This week's exercises emphasize relaxation, gentle stretching, and mindful breathing. You may notice fuller breathing, a looser body, and a quieter mind after practice. These changes often happen gradually.

Continue the same ten-minute routine each day at a comfortable pace. Some days you may feel energized, while others feel reflective or calm. Both experiences are valuable.

As the challenge comes to an end, take time to appreciate what you have done for your body and mind. Ten minutes a day is a meaningful commitment, with benefits that can extend beyond the exercise itself.

You are welcome to repeat the challenge, revisit favorite exercises, or continue practicing in a way that fits your life.

DAILY ROUTINE (10 MINUTES):

- **Centering Breath** | *Exercise 1, Chapter 5: Foundation and Posture (p. 16)*
- **Flowing River Hands** | *Exercise 23, Chapter 8: Calm and Breathing (p. 63)*
- **Seated Leg Extension** | *Exercise 17, Chapter 7: Strength and Flexibility (p. 50)*
- **Gentle Side Stretch** | *Exercise 35, Chapter 9: Joint Relief and Accessibility (p. 88)*
- **Breathing with the Ocean** | *Exercise 26, Chapter 8: Calm and Breathing (p. 69)*
- **Close the Circle** | *Exercise 27, Chapter 8: Calm and Breathing (p. 71)*

REFLECTION:

When you finish today's practice, sit or stand quietly for a moment. Notice how your body feels overall. Pay attention to your breathing, your posture, and your mood. Take a calm breath and recognize the sense of care you have given yourself today.

CHAPTER 16: AFTER THE 28 DAYS

You have reached the end of the 28-Day Gentle Tai Chi Challenge, and that is something worth acknowledging. Taking time each day to move, breathe, and care for your body is not always easy, and your commitment matters. Whether you followed the plan exactly or adjusted it along the way, completing this challenge shows that you are capable of creating a gentle, healthy routine that works for you.

This chapter is not about finishing Tai Chi, but about pausing to recognize what you have learned so far. Over the past four weeks, you have practiced moving more slowly, standing or sitting with better awareness, and listening to your body. These skills are just as important as the exercises themselves.

At this point, you'll notice small changes. Your balance will feel steadier, your movements will feel smoother, you'll feel calmer after practicing, and you'll be more confident in your ability to stay active. These changes often grow quietly over time, and they don't need to be dramatic to be meaningful.

For now, the most important next step is simple: keep moving in a way that feels comfortable and supportive. You might choose to repeat a favorite week from the challenge, practice a short routine every few days, or return to a few exercises that felt especially helpful. There is no correct schedule. Tai Chi works best when it fits naturally into your life.

You will also begin to notice which movements your body responds to the most. Some days you may prefer breathing and calming exercises, while other days gentle strength or balance work may feel right. Allowing yourself this choice helps keep the practice enjoyable and sustainable.

In the next part of this book, you will learn how to continue building on what you have started here. It will provide guidance on maintaining motivation, deepening your practice, and adapting Tai Chi to different stages of life. For now, take a moment to appreciate the effort you have made and the foundation you have created.

Your journey with Tai Chi is not ending here; it is simply opening into the next phase.

Part 4: Continuing the Journey

CARRYING TAI CHI INTO EVERYDAY LIFE

This fourth part of the book is about moving forward with confidence and ease. By now, Tai Chi is no longer something new; it has become a familiar way to care for your body, calm your mind, and stay connected to how you feel each day.

Part Four helps you continue your Tai Chi practice in a way that fits your life. There is no fixed schedule to follow and no finish line to reach. You will learn how to create your own short routines, revisit your favorite exercises, and gently adapt your practice as your needs change.

This section also explores how Tai Chi can support you beyond exercise. Simple breathing, mindful movement, and quiet awareness can be carried into daily activities like walking, resting, or handling stressful moments.

You are encouraged to trust yourself and move in ways that feel good and sustainable. Whether you continue practicing alone, with friends, or in a class, Tai Chi is something you can return to again and again.

This is not the end of your journey, but a steady beginning. Take what you have learned, move gently, and continue forward with calm, confidence, and care for your well-being.

CHAPTER 17: KEEP MOVING FORWARD

Completing this book and the 28-day challenge is an important milestone, but it's not the end of your Tai Chi journey. Think of it as a strong beginning. The movements, breathing, and awareness you have practiced are skills you can carry with you in many different ways for many years to come.

One of the most helpful things you can do after thirty days is to keep your practice simple. You don't need to add more time or learn complicated routines; ten minutes is enough. What matters is consistency and comfort. Some days you may feel energized and want to move a little longer. Other days, a few gentle movements and calm breathing may be all you need. Both are perfectly acceptable.

Creating your own ten-minute routine is a wonderful way to continue. Start with a centering breath to settle your body and mind. Choose three or four exercises you enjoyed or found helpful, such as a balance movement, a gentle stretch, and a flowing arm motion. End with a calming exercise to close your practice. Over time, you can naturally change this routine depending on how your body feels that day.

Tai Chi also works well alongside other gentle activities. Walking, light stretching, or chair-based yoga can complement your practice nicely. For example, a short walk followed by Tai Chi breathing can help you feel both energized and relaxed. If you already enjoy another activity, Tai Chi does not need to replace it. Instead, think of it as something that supports and enhances what you are already doing.

If you enjoy social connection, consider joining a Tai Chi class designed for seniors or beginners. Many community centers, senior centers, and online platforms offer gentle classes with seated options. Practicing with others can be motivating and enjoyable, but it's not required. Tai Chi can be just as meaningful when practiced alone, at home, in your own quiet space.

Most importantly, remember that this practice belongs to you. You are free to adapt it, pause it, or return to it whenever you choose. Continuing forward does not mean pushing harder; it means staying kind to your body and allowing movement to remain a supportive part of your life.

CHAPTER 18: LIVING THE TAI CHI WAY

Tai Chi is more than a set of exercises; it's a way of moving through daily life with greater calm, awareness, and ease. Even when you are not practicing the movements, the principles of Tai Chi continue to support you.

One of these principles is slowing down. In daily life, this might mean standing up more mindfully, taking a steady breath before walking, or pausing instead of rushing through tasks. Small moments of calm can make a noticeable difference in how your body and mind feel.

Breathing is another powerful tool you can carry with you. When you feel stressed, tired, or tense, return to the slow, gentle breathing you practiced in this book. A few steady breaths can help relax your shoulders, ease your thoughts, and bring your attention back to the present moment. You don't need to fix anything. Simply breathing with awareness is enough.

Practicing gratitude and awareness is also part of the Tai Chi way. This does not mean forcing positive thoughts. It simply means noticing what your body can do today. Perhaps you moved with less stiffness, stood a little taller, or felt calmer than before. These small acknowledgments help build confidence and appreciation over time.

Most importantly, remember that staying active does not require intensity. Gentle, regular movement supports balance, flexibility, and peace of mind. Tai Chi teaches that strength and softness can exist together. You can be strong without straining, and active without exhausting yourself.

As you continue forward, allow Tai Chi to meet you where you are. Your needs may change over time, and that is natural. What remains constant is your ability to choose movement, breathing, and awareness as tools for well-being.

Your Tai Chi journey does not have to look like anyone else's; it only needs to feel right to you. By moving gently, breathing calmly, and staying present, you are already living the Tai Chi way.

Part 5: Resources and Support

HELPFUL REFERENCES, REASSURANCE, AND TOOLS TO SUPPORT YOU ALONG THE WAY

This final part of the book is here to support you as you continue your Tai Chi journey beyond the exercises themselves. Think of it as a helpful reference section you can return to whenever you need guidance, reassurance, or a gentle reminder.

This section includes an easy-to-use exercise index and clear answers to common questions. You will also find a seated routine designed for days when your body needs extra rest.

You don't need to read this section all at once. You can flip to the part you need when you need it. Everything here is written to be straightforward, calm, and supportive, so you can feel confident and cared for as you continue moving, breathing, and staying active in your own way.

APPENDIX A: QUICK REFERENCE EXERCISE INDEX

This quick reference index is designed to help you easily find the exercises you need when you need them. You can use it to quickly look up movements by name, see what each one supports, and turn directly to the correct page. This section is especially helpful if you want to choose exercises based on how your body feels on a given day.

1. **Centering Breath (p. 16):** Calms the nervous system, improves breathing awareness, and prepares the body for movement.
2. **Mountain Stance (p. 18):** Improves posture, builds leg stability, and increases balance awareness.
3. **Seated Posture Alignment (p. 20):** Supports upright sitting, reduces back discomfort, and improves breathing.
4. **Shoulder Roll Release (p. 22):** Reduces shoulder and neck tension, and improves upper-body mobility.
5. **Open the Chest and Breathe (p. 24):** Encourages deeper breathing, improves posture, and releases chest tightness.
6. **Gentle Weight Shift (Left to Right) (p. 26):** Improves balance, strengthens the legs, and builds confidence in standing.
7. **Root Like a Tree (p. 28):** Enhances grounding, leg strength, and calm focus.
8. **Cloud Hands (p. 31):** Improves coordination, shoulder mobility, and relaxed flow.
9. **Wave the Hands Like Water (p. 33):** Releases shoulder tension and promotes smooth, flowing movement.
10. **Stepping Forward with Flow (p. 35):** Builds walking confidence and supports safe forward stepping.
11. **Brush Knee and Push (p. 37):** Improves coordination, balance, and controlled stepping.
12. **Parting the Wild Horse's Mane (p. 39):** Opens the chest, improves balance, and strengthens the upper back.
13. **Circle the Arms (Heaven and Earth Motion) (p. 41):** Improves shoulder flexibility and encourages gentle arm coordination.

14. **Turning the Waist (p. 43):** Reduces spinal stiffness and improves torso rotation for daily movement.
15. **Floating Hands Rising (p. 46):** Improves shoulder mobility, posture, and calm breathing.
16. **Lift and Lower the Heels (p. 48):** Strengthens the ankles and calves, and improves balance.
17. **Seated Leg Extension (p. 50):** Strengthens the thighs and knees, and supports standing and walking.
18. **The Archer's Pull (p. 52):** Strengthens the upper back, opens the chest, and improves posture.
19. **Row the Boat (p. 54):** Strengthens the core and back, and improves coordinated movement.
20. **Push the Mountain (p. 56):** Builds gentle arm strength and supports grounded stability.
21. **Opening the Flower (p. 58):** Opens the chest, improves arm flexibility, and encourages calm breathing.
22. **Holding the Ball (Qi Ball Breathing) (p. 61):** Calms the mind, improves breath control, and promotes relaxation.
23. **Flowing River Hands (p. 63):** Encourages smooth arm movement and calms the nervous system.
24. **Hands Like Clouds (Continuous Form) (p. 65):** Improves coordination, balance, and relaxed flow.
25. **Drawing Down the Sky (p. 67):** Supports deep breathing, full-body relaxation, and stress relief.
26. **Breathing with the Ocean (p. 69):** Regulates breathing rhythm, reduces tension, and promotes calm.
27. **Close the Circle (p. 71):** Grounds the body, calms the mind, and gently closes practice.
28. **Seated Mindful Breathing (p. 73):** Encourages deep relaxation, improves focus, and reduces anxiety.
29. **Seated Arm Flow (p. 76):** Improves arm circulation, shoulder mobility, and seated coordination.
30. **Gentle Neck Turns (p. 78):** Reduces neck stiffness and improves head and neck mobility.
31. **Wrist Circles and Finger Extensions (p. 80):** Improves hand flexibility, reduces stiffness, and supports daily hand use.

32. **Seated Side Bend Stretch (p. 82):** Stretches the side body and improves spinal flexibility while seated.
33. **Hip Circles (Standing or Seated) (p. 84):** Improves hip mobility and supports walking and balance.
34. **Knee Lifts with Support (p. 86):** Strengthens the legs and improves balance and knee control.
35. **Gentle Side Stretch (p. 88):** Improves side-body flexibility and reduces back tension.

You can return to this index anytime to quickly choose exercises that match your energy level, comfort, or goals for the day.

APPENDIX B: SEATED 10-MINUTE ROUTINE (FOR REST OR RECOVERY DAYS)

This seated routine is here for days when your body asks for something gentler. You might feel tired, sore, stiff, or simply in need of a calmer practice. Choosing this routine does not mean you are doing less or falling behind; it means you are listening to your body and responding with care.

Use this seated routine on recovery days, low-energy days, or anytime standing feels uncomfortable or unsafe. Tai Chi is about awareness and kindness toward yourself. Some days call for movement that is soft and supportive, and this routine was created with that in mind.

Find a sturdy chair with a flat seat and place both feet flat on the ground. Sit tall but relaxed. Take a moment to breathe slowly before you begin.

SEATED 10-MINUTE FLOW

Move through each exercise slowly and comfortably. You can shorten or lengthen any movement as needed.

1. **Seated Centering Breath:** Gently place your hands on your thighs. Breathe in through your nose and out through your mouth, feeling your chest and belly soften.
2. **Seated Arm Flow:** Lift your arms slowly as you inhale, then lower them as you exhale, moving like water.
3. **Gentle Neck Turns:** Slowly turn your head to one side, then the other, staying within a pain-free range.
4. **Seated Shoulder Sweep:** Raise one arm overhead and gently bend to the side, then switch sides.
5. **Wrist Circles and Finger Extensions:** Circle your wrists and gently open and close your fingers.
6. **Seated Leg Extension:** Extend one leg forward and lower it slowly, then switch legs.

7. **Close the Circle:** Bring your hands together near your chest and breathe calmly for a few moments.

Gentle Pacing Reminders

- Move slowly and smoothly.
- Rest whenever you need to.
- Focus on breathing rather than doing every movement perfectly.
- Stop immediately if you feel pain or dizziness.

This seated routine is a full Tai Chi practice. It supports circulation, joint comfort, and calm, and it helps you stay connected to your body even on quieter days.

APPENDIX C: FREQUENTLY ASKED QUESTIONS

This section answers some common concerns many seniors have when starting or continuing Tai Chi. If you ever feel unsure, you are not alone. These questions are normal, and there are no wrong reasons for asking them.

WHAT IF I CAN'T STAND FOR LONG PERIODS?

That's completely okay. The exercises in this book include seated options, and you can practice Tai Chi entirely from a chair if needed. Standing is not required to receive benefits. Balance, breathing, and gentle movement can all be practiced while seated.

CAN I DO TAI CHI IF I HAVE ARTHRITIS OR JOINT PAIN?

Yes, in most cases. Tai Chi is known for being gentle on the joints and can help reduce stiffness when done slowly and comfortably. Always stay within a pain-free range and avoid forcing movements. If you have severe pain or medical concerns, it's wise to check with your healthcare provider before starting.

HOW LONG BEFORE I SEE RESULTS?

Many people notice small changes within the first few weeks, such as feeling calmer, more relaxed, or slightly steadier. Physical improvements like better balance or flexibility often happen gradually. Tai Chi works best when practiced consistently and patiently.

DO I NEED SPECIAL EQUIPMENT OR CLOTHING?

No special equipment is needed. Comfortable clothing that allows you to move freely is enough. Flat, supportive shoes or bare feet are fine. A sturdy chair and a small open space are all you need.

WHAT IF I MISS A DAY OR FALL BEHIND?

Missing a day does not undo your progress. Tai Chi is not about perfection or strict schedules. Simply return when you are ready. Even a few minutes of gentle movement is beneficial.

IS IT NORMAL TO FEEL AWKWARD AT FIRST?

Yes. Learning new movements can feel unfamiliar, especially at the beginning. With time, the exercises will feel more natural. Be patient with yourself and focus on how the movement feels rather than how it looks.

Tai Chi is meant to support you, not stress you. Move at your own pace, trust your body, and remember that small steps truly matter.

Conclusion: A Note from the Author

Thank you for taking the time with yourself and this book. Choosing to move, breathe, and care for your body is a meaningful decision at any age, and it deserves recognition.

Aging brings changes, but it does not take away your ability to grow stronger, calmer, or more connected to your body. Gentle movement can still bring comfort, confidence, and quiet joy. Every breath you take with awareness and every movement you do with care is a positive step.

There is no "right" way to practice Tai Chi. Some days will feel easier than others. Some days you may move more slowly or choose to rest. All of that is part of a healthy relationship with your body. Progress does not always look dramatic; it manifests as feeling steadier, sleeping a little better, or moving with less fear.

Please remember that your effort matters. Even on days when you do very little, choosing awareness is still a form of practice. Tai Chi is something you can return to again and again, whenever you need calm, balance, or reassurance.

It's never too late to move gently, breathe deeply, and care for yourself. Thank you for allowing this practice to be a part of your journey.

Thanks for Reading!

Thank you for choosing *Gentle Tai Chi for Seniors*. I'm truly honored to have been a small part of your journey toward better balance, strength, and peace of mind.

My hope in writing this book was simple: to make movement feel safe, achievable, and kind to your body, no matter where you're starting from. Tai Chi doesn't ask you to move fast or push through pain. It invites you to slow down, breathe deeply, and reconnect with your body in a way that feels calm and empowering. Even a few minutes a day can make a meaningful difference.

If these routines helped you feel a little steadier on your feet, a little looser in your joints, or a little more confident in your movements, then this book has done exactly what it was meant to do.

Please remember that progress doesn't have to be big to be valuable. Every gentle movement, every mindful breath, is a step toward long-term well-being.

Your feedback truly matters. If you found this book helpful, I would be so grateful if you'd consider leaving an honest review.

Your words can help other seniors feel confident choosing a gentle, supportive path to staying active. You can share your thoughts by using the QR code included in this book.

Thank you again for trusting me to guide you through these routines. Be patient with yourself, move at your own pace, and keep honoring your body with care and compassion.

Wishing you continued balance, comfort, and calm, one gentle movement at a time.

With gratitude,

Hannah Harmony

References

Chen, W., Li, M., Li, H., Lin, Y., & Feng, Z. (2023). "Tai Chi for Fall Prevention and Balance Improvement in Older Adults: A Systematic Review and Meta-analysis of Randomized Controlled Trials." *Frontiers in Public Health*, 11. https://doi.org/10.3389/fpubh.2023.1236050

Leung, L. Y. L., Tam, H. L., & Ho, J. K. M. (2022). "Effectiveness of Tai Chi on Older Adults: A Systematic Review of Systematic Reviews with Re-meta-analysis." *Archives of Gerontology and Geriatrics*, 103, 104796. https://doi.org/10.1016/j.archger.2022.104796

Nan, L., Grunberg, D., Silva, S. D., & Divya Sivaramakrishnan. (2024). "Evaluating the Effectiveness of Tai Chi in Short-Term, Medium-Term, and Long-Term on Balance and Strength among the Elderly: A Systematic Review and Meta-Analysis." *Archives of Gerontology and Geriatrics Plus*, 100080–100080. https://doi.org/10.1016/j.aggp.2024.100080

Ting, W. (2015). *Essential Concepts of Tai Chi*. Xlibris Corporation.

Yang, F.-C., Desai, A. B., Esfahani, P., Sokolovskaya, T. V., & Bartlett, D. J. (2021). "Effectiveness of Tai Chi for Health Promotion of Older Adults: A Scoping Review of Meta-Analyses." *American Journal of Lifestyle Medicine*, 16 (6), 700–716. https://doi.org/10.1177/15598276211001291

About the Author

Hannah Harmony is a lifelong wellness educator and movement enthusiast dedicated to helping older adults stay active, confident, and pain-free through gentle daily practice. After years of teaching balance, breathing, and body-awareness techniques to seniors in community centers and wellness retreats, she developed a simple approach to Tai Chi that anyone can follow, no matter their age or experience level.

Her method focuses on small, consistent movements that restore coordination, relieve joint stiffness, and build inner strength. Hannah believes it's never too late to move with grace and vitality, and her 28-day program is designed to make that transformation achievable in just ten minutes a day.

When she's not teaching or writing, Hannah enjoys peaceful walks at sunrise, tending her garden, and practicing mindfulness, the same calm and balance she hopes to bring into the lives of her readers.